Science in a Social Context

# The Atomic Bomb

**Margaret Gowing**
*Professor of History of Science,*
*University of Oxford*

**and**

**Lorna Arnold**
*Assistant Historian,*
*UK Atomic Energy Authority*

Butterworths

LONDON · BOSTON
Sydney · Wellington · Durban · Toronto

The Butterworth Group

United Kingdom    Butterworth & Co (Publishers) Ltd
London    88 Kingsway, WC2B 6AB

Australia    Butterworths Pty Ltd
Sydney    586 Pacific Highway, Chatswood, NSW 2067
Also at Melbourne, Brisbane, Adelaide and Perth

Canada    Butterworth & Co (Canada) Ltd
Toronto    2265 Midland Avenue,
Scarborough, Ontario, M1P 4S1

New Zealand    Butterworths of New Zealand Ltd
Wellington    T & W Young Building,
77—85 Customhouse Quay, 1, CPO Box 472

South Africa    Butterworth & Co (South Africa) (Pty) Ltd
Durban    152—154 Gale Street

USA    Butterworth (Publishers) Inc
Boston    19 Cummings Park, Woburn, Mass. 01801



© SISCON 1979
First published 1979
ISBN 0 408 71311 9

British Library Cataloguing in Publication Data

Gowing, Margaret
   The atomic bomb.
   1. Atomic weapons — Social aspects
   I. Title    II. Arnold, Lorna    III. Science in a
Social Context (Project)
   301.5'93    UF767    78—41269

   ISBN 0-408-71311-9

Typeset by Butterworth Litho Preparation Department
Printed in England by Billing and Sons Ltd,
Guildford and London

# Chapter One
# Introduction

It was one of the most fateful coincidences of history that the discovery of atomic fission came in the same year as the outbreak of the Second World War. The discovery of the effects of splitting an atom of the heavy element, uranium — a material hitherto considered pretty worthless — came around the New Year of 1939. It was found that in uranium fission energy was released on the enormous scale of Einstein's famous equation $E = mc^2$. That is *Energy = mass x (speed of light)$^2$*.

Could the energy be harnessed? Could it be used for peaceful purposes — electric power — or for weapons of war? Or both? Atomic energy was indeed to prove dual-purpose. The atomic reactors of the future which were built to produce electricity might also simultaneously produce material usable for atomic weapons. This was suspected in 1939 even though scientific and technological understanding of the processes was very incomplete. The full implications of this duality were not understood for another 30 years or so. For a long time atomic energy seemed to have two distinct sides: one good, and one bad. The good side was the prospect of almost unlimited energy supplies since 1 lb of uranium (roughly an inch cube), if fully converted to energy*, would be equivalent to 1350 tons of coal or 5000 barrels of crude oil. However the bad side, atomic weapons, was uppermost in scientists' minds as war approached in 1939.

The subsequent production of two atomic bombs in the Second World War did not affect the outcome of the war although, by shortening it, the bombs probably reduced the total number of casualties. But the bombs were one of the land-marks of history. The world could never be the same again. Listed below are some of the profound changes brought by the atomic age:

1. Mankind was soon to acquire the power to destroy civilized life on earth. Atomic bombs using nuclear fission could cause the most terrible devastation but would probably not eliminate life since there was a scientific limit to their size. However in the wartime atomic bomb laboratory at Los Alamos in the United States, work had begun on the hydrogen bomb in which energy was released not by splitting atoms of heavy elements but by fusing atoms of light elements. There was no theoretical limit to the size of such a weapon.

2. Science had become indissolubly involved in the life and death of nations. Scientists — in particular the physicists — became deeply implicated in national and international politics.

* It is not yet known how to convert uranium completely.

3. Little science had become big science. The alliance of 'pure' theoretical and experimental scientists with applied scientists and engineers
   and technological administrators had, within five years, transformed
   a tentative improbable idea into a vast project costing two thousand
   million dollars which produced two bombs which killed over a
   quarter of a million and fearfully injured many more.
4. The horror of the atomic bombs made the scientists, even more than
   other people, especially eager to develop atomic power which was
   viewed as an unmixed blessing.
5. The outcome of the wartime project raised expectations that any
   practical technological objective that was also scientifically possible
   could be achieved if sufficient resources and effort were devoted to it.
6. Before the war the total stock of separated radioactive material in
   the world consisted of three kilograms of radium. The atomic
   projects of the war-time and post-war worlds produced large
   quantities of radioactive materials, some of them very dangerous
   and some of them, such as plutonium 239, with very long radioactive half-lives.

Thus in 1980, hardly more than 40 years after the discovery of
uranium fission, the world annual output of plutonium will, it is
estimated, be 65 tonnes; the total production 1972–1980 will be
249 tonnes. Plutonium, which is made in nuclear reactors, does not
occur in nature; it is one of the most unpleasant substances known to
man, and in one form has a half-life of 24 000 years. Storage of radioactive materials for periods as long as those separating us from the last
Ice Age imports a new time-scale into human experience.

Discussion classes may think of other profound changes.


## Scope of course

A brief course cannot cover the atom bomb, and the subsequent
hydrogen bomb, from its origins to the present day. So this book
concentrates (after a look at the pre-history) on the crucial 14 years,
1939–1953. In 1939 atomic weapon research began; in 1945 two
atomic bombs were dropped on Japan; in 1949 came Russia's first
fission bomb test and the United States' first test of a large thermonuclear device; in 1953 Russia tested her first thermonuclear weapon.

Primarily British, and to a lesser extent United States, developments
in this period are discussed, mainly because of the accessibility of the
literature in the United Kingdom. The US story is much more important
than the British, and a great deal has been published about it. The
reading list includes both American and British books. Many of the
references are to Gowing's books because they are all still available and
cover most, though not all, of the topics dealt with.

The other countries which had a potential interest in atomic bombs at some time in this 14 year period were Canada, France, Germany, Japan and USSR. Brief references are made to all these countries in the course except for Japan, for which there is little accessible literature (but see Weiner, 1978).

Chapter 2    *Prehistory* covers the developments of physics which led to the discovery of atomic fission and the belief that atomic energy could be released for electric power or a bomb.

Chapter 3    *The Atomic Bomb and World War Two* covers the development of the atomic bombs that fell on Japan, and touches on comparable work in Germany and Russia.

Chapter 4    *The Atomic Bomb and the Postwar World* looks at the new problems of atomic energy in the formative years from 1945 to 1953.

## Basic reading list

In the course time available, students' reading must be highly selective. In each of the chapters therefore numerous page references are given from books in the basic reading list below. Books are listed in alphabetical order by author's name, and will be referred to hereafter by author's name and date of publication. The most important books are indicated by two stars, other useful books by one star.
    Students are recommended to begin by reading a basic technical background which is available in:

Asimov (1975), pp. 469–478
Gowing (1974), Vol 1, pp. 451–464 or ⎱ the same appendix
Gowing (1974), Vol 2, pp. 506–519    ⎰ reproduced in both volumes
Patterson (1976), pp. 23–49

More technical accounts are to be found in Sherfield (1972), pp. 7–33.

Asimov, I. (1975). *Guide to Science*, 1 The Physical Sciences. Pelican.
*Barnaby, F. (1977), 'Hiroshima and Nagasaki: the survivors'. *New Scientist*, 25 August 1977.
*Beyerchen, A. D. (1977). *Scientists under Hitler*, Yale University Press.
Clark, R. W. (1961). *The Birth of the Bomb*. Horizon Press.
*Clark, R. W. (1965). *Tizard*. Methuen.
*Clark, R. W. (1973). *Einstein*. Hodder.
Clark, R. W. (1975). *Bertrand Russell*. Cape & Weidenfeld & Nicholson.

*Compton, A. H. (1956). *Atomic Quest: a Personal Narrative.* Oxford University Press.

Eggleston, W. (1965). *Canada's Nuclear Story.* Clarke Irwin.

Fermi, Laura (1954). *Atoms in the Family; My Life with Enrico Fermi.* Chicago University Press.

**Fleming, D. and Bailyn, B. (1969). *The Intellectual Migration.* Harvard University Press.

Goldschmidt, B. (1962). *L'Aventure Atomique.* Fayard.

Goldschmidt, B. (1967). *Les Rivalités Atomiques.* Fayard.

Goldsmith, M. (1976). *Frédéric Joliot-Curie: a Biography.* Lawrence and Wishart.

Goudsmit, S. A. (1947). *Alsos.* Henry Schuman Inc.

**Gowing, M. (1964). *Britain and Atomic Energy 1939–1945.* Macmillan.

**Gowing, M. (1974). *Independence and Deterrence: Britain and Atomic Energy 1945–1952, Vol 1, Policy Making, Vol 2, Policy Execution.* Macmillan.

*Greenberg, D. S. (1969). *The Politics of American Science.* Penguin.

Groom, A. J. R. (1974). *British Thinking about Nuclear Weapons.* Francis Pinter.

*Groueff, S. (1967). *Manhattan Project: the untold story of the making of the bomb.* Little, Brown & Co.

*Groves, L. R. (1962). *Now it Can be Told: the story of the Manhattan Project.* Harper & Brothers.

**Hewlett, R. G. and Anderson, O. E. (1962). *A History of the United States Atomic Energy Commission, Vol I, The New World.* Pennsylvania State University Press.

*Hewlett, R. G. (1974). *Nuclear Navy 1946–1968.* University of Chicago Press.

**Hewlett, R. G. and Duncan, F. (1969). *A History of the United States Atomic Energy Commission, Vol II, Atomic Shield.* Pennsylvania State University Press.

**Irving, D. (1967). *The Virus House: Germany's Atomic Research and Allied Counter-Measures.* William Kimber.

Jungk, R. (1970). *Brighter than a Thousand Suns.* Pelican.

Kramish, A. (1959). *Atomic Energy in the Soviet Union.* Stanford University Press.

Lilienthal, D. E. (1963). *Change, Hope and the Bomb.* Princeton University Press.

Lilienthal, D. E. (1964). *The Journals of David E. Lilienthal, Vol II, The Atomic Energy Years 1945–50.* Harper & Row.

*Major, J. (1971). *The Oppenheimer Hearing.* Batsford.

Mendelssohn, K. (1973). *The World of Walther Nernst.* Macmillan.

Modelski, G. A. (1959). *Atomic Energy in the Communist Bloc.* Melbourne University Press.

Moorehead, A. (1952). *The Traitors.* Hamish Hamilton.

*Moss, N. (1970). *Men who Play God: the Story of the Hydrogen Bomb.* Penguin.

Oliphant, M. (1972). *Rutherford — Recollections of the Cambridge Days.* Elsevier Publishing.

Patterson, W. C. (1976). *Nuclear Power.* Penguin.

**Pierre, A. (1972). *Nuclear Politics: the British Experience with an Independent Strategic Force 1939–1970.* Oxford University Press.

Scheinman, L. (1965). *Atomic Energy Policy in France under the Fourth Republic.* Princeton University Press.

Schonland, B. (1968). *The Atomists 1805–1933.* Clarendon Press.

*Sherfield, Lord (1972). *Economic and Social Consequences of Nuclear Energy.* Oxford University Press.

Sherwin, M. J. (1975). *A World Destroyed: The Atomic Bomb and the Grand Alliance.* Alfred A. Knopf, New York.

Smith, A. Kimball (1965). *A Peril and a Hope.* University of Chicago Press.

Smyth, H. D. (1945). *Atomic Energy.* Government Printing Office USA and HMSO, London 1945.

*Stern, P. M. (1971). *The Oppenheimer Case.* Hart-Davies.

Strauss, L. (1962). *Men and Decisions.* Doubleday & Co.

*Truman, H. S. (1955). *Memoirs — Vol I, Year of Decisions.* Doubleday & Co. also Hodder & Stoughton.

**USAEC (1971). *In the Matter of J. Robert Oppenheimer.* M.I.T. Press.

Weart, S. R. (1975). 'Scientists with a Secret', *Physics Today,* **29,** 2.

Weiner, C. (1978). 'Nuclear Weapons History: Japan's Wartime Bomb Projects Revealed', *Science,* Vol. 199, 13 January 1978.

**Wilson, J. (ed.) (1975). *All in Our Time. The Reminiscences of Twelve Nuclear Pioneers,* The Bulletin of the Atomic Scientists.

**York, H. (1976). *The Advisors: Oppenheimer, Teller and the Super Bomb.* W. H. Freeman & Co.


## Notes on reading list

The basic books are the official histories of the British and American projects: Gowing (1964) and (1974), Hewlett and Anderson (1962), Hewlett and Duncan (1969). *Atomic Energy,* Smyth (1945) was the official account of the 'Manhattan Project', subtitled *A General Account of the Development of Methods of Using Atomic Energy for Military Purposes under the Auspices of the United States Government,* issued in August 1945, only a few days after the first atomic bombs had been dropped at Hiroshima and Nagasaki. It was at the time a very full account of the scientific and technological background to this event. Clark (1961) was written from oral memories 20 years old and was largely superseded by the British official history, Gowing (1964), written with full access to the records. Pierre (1972) is excellent and Groom (1974), though overlong and deficient in interpretation, contains much useful material.

Accounts of the US project are given by Groueff (1967), Groves (1962), and Jungk (1970). Groves's is based on his personal experience in charge of the project. Jungk's is readable but 'hopelessly inaccurate' according to Hewlett and Anderson (1962) p. 662. A recent US paperback, Wilson (1975), contains vivid first-hand accounts of the wartime project. The personal and political relationships of the American scientists and problems of security are revealed above all in the famous Oppenheimer hearings. These have been reprinted in USAEC (1971). The books by Major (1971), and Stern (1971) also cover the case. York (1976) is extremely good about these relationships and about both the US decision to make an H-bomb and the comparison of US and Russian progress in the 1950s. Kimball Smith (1965) describes the American scientists' movement for political control of atomic energy.

For security and atomic spies in Britain see Gowing (1974) Vol 2, Chapter 16, and Moorehead (1952).

The German project is described by Irving (1967), and by Goudsmit (1947). Irving's views on German progress and why Germany failed to produce a bomb are controversial. The Canadian project is described by Gowing (1964) and (1974), and by Eggleston (1965). The French project is described by Goldschmidt (1962) and (1967), Goldsmith (1976) and Scheinman (1965), and in part by Gowing (1964) and (1974). There is some, but not much, information about the Russian project in Kramish (1959), Modelski (1959) and York (1976).

# Chapter Two
# Prehistory

Atomic theory grew out of chemistry as much as physics. If anyone can be called the father of modern atomic theory it was John Dalton, the Manchester chemist, in his work at the beginning of the 19th century. Rutherford, whom we think of as a very great physicist, received his Nobel prize for chemistry; Hahn and Strassmann who, at the end of 1938, discovered the effects of splitting an atom of uranium, were chemists.

Nevertheless an intensely exciting, revolutionary, new period of physics was opening at the end of the 19th century, which culminated in the discovery of atomic fission at the turn of 1938/39. Remarkable advances were made in experimental atomic physics and, during the inter-war years, in theory; this was the new quantum mechanics. Physicists remember this as an immensely exhilarating period: the international physics community was very small with, according to Sir Nevill Mott, only 30 or so theoretical physicists, and there were so many obvious problems to be tackled that research easily yielded rich returns. Research was also very cheap, with simple apparatus (see Oliphant (1972), pp. 38–42) although already in 1930 Ernest Lawrence in California had developed the cyclotron, the first big accelerator. A summary of the progressive understanding of atoms and their structure is available in Gowing (1964), pp. 3–30.

Some of the important points to notice in this story are:
1. How often the discovery of fission was missed in the 1930s, and why.
2. The method of communicating the news of the discovery of fission by Hahn and Strassmann in Germany at the end of 1938. Even before it was published the news spread rapidly — by letter from Hahn to his former colleague, Lise Meitner, then a refugee in Sweden; by word of mouth from her to her physicist nephew, Otto Frisch, who was on a Christmas visit from Copenhagen; from him to the great Danish physicist, Niels Bohr. He announced the news to a conference of physicists in the USA in January 1939.
3. The competitive rush by scientists of different countries to confirm and follow up the discovery of fission. French physicists were the first to discover, in April 1939, the possibility of a chain reaction. They showed that in fission not only was an immense amount of energy released but also spare neutrons, which flew off to split other atoms, releasing more and more energy and neutrons.
4. Some scientists, conscious of commercial possibilities, took out patents on their work: this was true of Fermi's group in Italy (Gowing, 1964, p. 22); the French physicists (Goldsmith, 1976, pp. 75, 142; Gowing, 1964, pp. 52, 74–76). Szilard took out a

patent in 1933 when he realised the possibility of a chain reaction
and its military potential and he gave it to the British Admiralty
(Fleming and Bailyn, 1969, pp. 101–2, 106).

It is sometimes suggested that until the outbreak of the Second
World War, science and scientists were essentially 'pure' and non-
political. This is untrue because science and politics had constantly
intermingled over the centuries and in the inter-war period science,
especially physics, became deeply involved in politics. This was so in
the 1920s before the advent of the Nazis in Germany. Einstein's relativity
theory had been bitterly attacked, even by scientists, because of racial
and nationalist antipathy to Einstein as a person (see Beyerchen, 1977,
Fleming and Bailyn, 1969, p. 207, and Jungk, 1970, p. 43). The extra-
ordinarily talented group of Hungarian Jewish scientists was already
being driven into exile (Fleming and Bailyn, 1969, pp. 6, 712, 714, 716).
Some writers have linked the great creativity of German physics in the
1920s with the unsettled post-war life there (Mendelssohn, 1973, and
Jungk, 1970). With the advent of the Nazis to power the great intellectual migration of scientific and other talent from Germany began.
The numbers were not very great but the quality was very high. The
refugee scientists were to be especially prominent in the wartime
atomic bomb program in the US and Britain (Fleming and Bailyn,
1969, chapters 2 & 4). Scientific and political tumult went together in
the inter-war years.

How far did scientists foresee the consequences of their atomic
discoveries? Until the spring of 1939 very few seriously appreciated the
possibilities. In 1933 Rutherford made his well-known remark that
expectations of sources of power from atomic transmutations were
'merest moonshine' but earlier in the century he had foreseen the
possibilities. (Oliphant, 1972, chapter 10 and Gowing, 1974, p. 1).
So had his far-sighted colleague Soddy who had discovered with
Rutherford the nature of radioactivity and, on his own, radioisotopes.
J. B. S. Haldane, the biologist, had been sceptical about atomic energy
but after the discovery of nuclear fission was quick to see the possibilities, though prepared to bet against the immediate success of the
experiments going on in several countries.

The prescient and somewhat maverick Hungarian refugee physicist*,
Leo Szilard, has given a dramatic account† of his own sudden realization
in 1933 that an atomic bomb was feasible.

Writers of fiction appreciated the coming events perhaps more
clearly than anyone else. In 1914 H. G. Wells predicted, in *The World
Set Free,* the discovery in 1933 of a neutral particle which was the key
to the nuclear chain reaction. He was only a year out! He described the

* After the Second World War he turned to biology and was also a pioneer in
information science.

† Appendix 1

10

introduction of atomic energy in 1953, causing a new industrial revolution: then in 1956 a global war in which the atomic bomb was 'the crowning triumph of military science, the ultimate explosive'. He even thought of fall-out. But it should be noted that his book was dedicated to Soddy's work *Interpretation of Radium**. Olaf Stapledon in 1930, in *Last and First Men*, placed the discovery of atomic energy in AD 2000 and described an atomic explosion with fireball and mushroom cloud, and in 1932 the author politician Harold Nicholson in an uncannily prophetic novel, *Public Faces*, foresaw the atomic bomb. 'It is surprising', wrote Dr. A Michaelis†, 'how often the trained imagination of writers, when brought to bear on scientific facts which are not yet exploited by technology, can approach the truth'.

The discovery by the French physicists in April 1939 that a chain reaction in uranium was possible brought a general realization of the potentialities of atomic energy. The Frenchmen were primarily impressed by the hope of nuclear power, so much so that, as we saw, they took out several patents. Elsewhere, fears about the real possibility of an atomic bomb were voiced. Again the most dramatic statement is that of Szilard‡, who was by this time working in the United States. Scientists in Britain and the United States approached their governments on the subject. In the spring of 1939, the American scientist Dean Pegram introduced Enrico Fermi to an Admiral in the US Navy who asked him to keep the naval authorities informed of the possibilities of a uranium super-bomb (Gowing, 1964, p. 34; Hewlett and Anderson, 1962, p. 15). In Britain, two famous physicists** urged action to preempt the valuable supplies of uranium in the Belgian Congo; enquiries about it were made, but no action was taken to buy it. Another scientist, Sir Henry Tizard, believed the odds against successful military application were 100 000 to 1, but this single chance was too important to ignore. Preliminary research began at Imperial College, London.

Accounts of the advances of nuclear physics were available for all to read right up to the outbreak of war. In the summer of 1939, a group of American scientists led by Szilard tried to hold back publication of information of potential military significance (Sherwin, 1975, pp. 22—25; Hewlett and Anderson, 1962, pp. 25—26; Fleming and Bailyn, 1969, pp. 109—110; Weart, 1975). But it was still peacetime and a scientific vow of secrecy could not be imposed. The curtain of silence only came down when war broke out.

---

* We are indebted for this clue to M. I. Freedman of John Hopkins University.
† 'How Nuclear Energy was Foretold', *New Scientist*, 1 March 1962.
‡ Appendix 2.
** L. Bragg and G. P. Thomson.

## Reading

ESSENTIAL

Fleming and Bailyn (1969), chapters 2 and 4.
Gowing (1964), pp. 3–37.
Hewlett and Anderson (1962), pp. 1–20.
Wilson ed. (1975), chapter 1.


ADDITIONAL

Beyerchen (1977).
Clark (1961), chapters 1, 2 & 3.
Irving (1967), pp. 11–39.
Jungk (1970).
Mendelssohn (1973).
Schonland (1968).
Weart (1975).

### Points for discussion or essays

1. Is the fact that fission was missed so often  a unique phenomenon in the history of science, or is it a significant example of the way scientists think and work?
2. What difference did the timing of the discovery of uranium fission make to the world?
3. Discuss the pros and cons of an appeal for secrecy among scientists in the summer of 1939.
4. What meaning do you think the word 'pure' has when applied to atomic physics in the 1930s?
5. What conclusions about the internationalism of science can you draw from nuclear physics in the 1930s?

# Chapter Three
# The Atomic Bomb and World War Two

This chapter is primarily concerned with the events which led to the
dropping of the two atomic bombs on Japan — that is, with events
in Britain and the United States and, to a lesser extent, in France and
Canada. The bombs were manufactured in the United States but the
vast size and importance of the US project have concealed the fact that
the bomb was 'invented' in Britain.

## The study of feasibility and the British contribution

To take first the early British work. By the early days of the war
scepticism had replaced the sense of urgency about atomic research.
This was largely because of the paper by Bohr and Wheeler published
two days before the war began. For this had shown that fission is far
more likely to occur in certain uranium atoms — in U235 — than in
other uranium atoms — in U238. Natural uranium from the earth
consists 99.3% of U238 atoms and only 0.7% of U235 atoms. If a chain
reaction in natural uranium is to succeed it is necessary to moderate or
slow down the neutrons, but this does not result in the fantastically
fast reaction needed for a bomb. Few scientists saw clearly that to
make a uranium bomb it is essential to have a chain reaction with fast
or unmoderated neutrons, which is only possible with a lump of U235.
The few who did see this still dismissed atom bombs as impracticable
because it seemed an impossible task to separate the U235 from the
U238 atoms: they are almost identical chemically and the difference
between them for practical purposes is simply that a 235 atom is of
slightly lower mass.

Then in the spring of 1940 two refugee scientists in Birmingham —
Otto Frisch, who had been one of the 'discoverers' of fission early in
1939, and Rudolf Peierls, a distinguished theoretical physicist — wrote
a memorandum of crucial importance. They showed, first, that a lump
of pure U235 would give a sufficiently quick chain reaction for a bomb.
Secondly they proposed an industrial method for separating U235.
Thirdly they foretold the horrors an atom bomb would bring and saw
the strategic and moral implications — whether, for example, a bomb
should be used. A 5 kg bomb, they said, would liberate the energy of
several thousand tons of dynamite and would besides cause radiation
which would be fatal to living beings long after the explosion. The
Frisch—Peierls memorandum* with its clear grasp of principles and

* Appendix 3. This memorandum 'on the properties of a radioactive superbomb',
  which is taken from Clark (1965), pp. 214—217, was accompanied by the more
  technical memorandum 'on the construction of a super-bomb' reproduced in
  Gowing (1964), pp. 389—393.

properties is a remarkable example of scientific insight. The two
scientists had performed one of the most difficult tasks in science —
they had asked the right questions.

The Frisch—Peierls memorandum was sent through Sir Henry
Tizard to G. P. Thomson who took it to the Committees on the
Scientific Survey of Air Defence and of Air Warfare. Interest, which
had been waning, now waxed rapidly. The British set up the Maud
Committee, one of the most successful committees this country has
ever seen, and under its wing research proceeded with great urgency.
Refugee scientists excluded for reasons of secrecy from other war
work were very prominent in the work on the atom bomb, the greatest
of war secrets. This was to be true in the United States also.

France fell in the summer of 1940. The work of the Maud Committee, which had not yet got very far, was reinforced by the dramatic
arrival of two French scientists, Dr. H. von Halban and Dr. L. Kowarski,
members of the team which had reported early in 1939 on the possibility of a slow chain reaction in U238, whose work seemed to
promise not bombs but the hope of nuclear power. With them the two
French physicists brought 26 five-litre cans of heavy water — the total
world stock — from Norway; this heavy water was important because
it was the most efficient moderator for slowing down neutrons.

The Maud Committee settled the French scientists at the Cavendish
Laboratory at Cambridge. Here two colleagues† predicted that in the
course of slow chain reactions in U238 a new element, almost completely unknown in nature, would be formed, which would behave like
U235 and would be usable for bombs. They called this element
plutonium.

It was the arrival of the French scientists that gave the British a
head start at the end of the war in designing and constructing slow
neutron reactors to produce both plutonium for bombs and also
nuclear power.

The Maud Committee reported in the summer of 1941 showing
lucidly and with great cogency how and why an atomic bomb was
possible, certainly with U235 and possibly with plutonium. The
politicians then came into the business and gave the project the go-
ahead  But now the big question arose. Was it possible to build the
enormous plant in Britain, which was being bombed and where man-
power was very scarce? Would it be better to shift the project to
North America.

What had been happening in the United States? It must be remem-
bered that the United States was neutral in the war until Japan attacked
Pearl Harbour in December 1941. In October 1939 two refugee scientists, one of them Szilard, drafted a letter to President Roosevelt* to be
signed by Einstein (another refugee) about the possibility of atomic

† E. Bretscher and N. Feather.

* Appendix 4.

14

bombs and the danger that the Nazis might develop the bomb first. As a result research began in the US, but it was desultory, and the neutral American scientists told the British loftily in 1940 that it would be a sheer waste of time for them to study uranium as a war investigation. The US scientists did important work including the separation of plutonium early in 1941 and the isolation, in August 1942, of the first visible amount of pure plutonium. But they did not ask the leading scientific questions nor put their jigsaw pieces together into a whole. Only when they read the brilliant British Maud Report, which was given to them in the late summer of 1941, did they take the project seriously and persuade their government to set up what became the huge Manhattan Project. Without the British work the Second World War would almost certainly have ended before an atomic bomb was dropped.

When the British scientists and politicians discussed whether their atomic plants should be built at home or in North America they were divided. It was finally decided that the first pilot plant must be built in Britain while the later full scale plants should be built in North America, probably in Canada. The reluctance to shift the project to North America had deep roots — for example, in the belief that whoever possessed such a plant would be able to dictate terms to the rest of the world. At this stage, the autumn of 1941, the Americans, conscious that the British were so far ahead, proposed a jointly-controlled Anglo-American project. But the proposal was treated very coolly, and indeed the British missed the bus. For the Americans launched an all-out effort to make an atomic bomb even before Pearl Harbour, in December 1941, totally committed them to the war. Within six months the US project had far outstripped the British effort. British failure to foresee this profoundly affected the future of Britain's project. If the two projects had become closely intertwined in 1941 when the British were well ahead they could not easily have been pulled apart again.

In mid-1942 the British realized that the Americans were forging ahead very fast, while they themselves had the greatest difficulty in constructing even a few pilot units of a plant for separating U235. The technological gap became, for the first time, painfully obvious. The British now wanted desperately to get into the project on terms of equal partnership, because they realized that they could not proceed on their own, but the Americans now did not want them. Only after a great struggle, and after nearly a year of total breakdown in collaboration, did Churchill and Roosevelt sign the Quebec Agreement* of August 1943, which enabled the British to participate in the US project and which led to joint purchase of uranium. The Agreement had two other important provisions: that neither side would use the bomb against third parties without the other's consent, and that neither country

* Appendix 5.

would communicate any atomic information to third parties except by mutual consent. After the Quebec Agreement was signed all the physicists working on U235 and fast neutron bomb calculations in Britain joined the US project.

Meanwhile the Anglo-French slow neutron team from Cambridge had gone to Canada. The US government disliked the Free French and had made it clear that they did not want the team. Canada, simply to help Britain, agreed to provide facilities. After early difficulties the project flourished and Canada, then a small nation with very limited scientific resources, became by accident of war one of the first countries to be involved in nuclear power. Her current successful heavy water reactors come in direct descent from the prewar work of the French, via the two French scientists who brought the heavy water to England in 1940.

Britain's native project had now virtually closed down for the war and its scientists had migrated to North America. They were to be found in several, but not all, parts of the US project: the biggest contingent was at Los Alamos where the atom bomb was fabricated, but no British scientists were admitted to the US reactors where plutonium was produced. In the end the British were the junior partners in the atomic project they had launched. Their contribution was small compared with the US effort but was of key importance in certain crucial areas.


## The Manhattan Project

After reading the Maud Report the Americans reorganised their uranium project. Renamed the Manhattan Project in June 1942, it was to be run by the US Army, partly because of the huge scale of construction and partly to ensure the utmost secrecy. Little more than three years later a vast continent-wide complex of completely innovatory plants had been conceived, designed, built and operated; two kinds of fissile material — U235 and plutonium, the new man-made element — had been produced; two types of atom bomb had been designed and fabricated, and one tested; Hiroshima and Nagasaki had been destroyed each by a single weapon. The project was extraordinary proof of US ascendancy in technology, engineering, industrial capacity and large-scale organization.

Yet as late as the end of 1944 the whole program was riddled with uncertainties and success was still doubtful. A massive effort had to be devoted to one step alone — producing the fissile material. Since no one method was proven all methods were explored: four routes to U235 and also the production of plutonium, which required the construction not only of the first nuclear reactors but also of a chemical separation plant. The fabrication and design of the bomb involved

complex processes and the most abstruse physical calculations. The
bomb work was concentrated under the direction of Robert Oppenheimer
at Los Alamos in New Mexico, chosen for its extremely remote location.
In this land of extinct volcanoes a galaxy of many of the world's most
brilliant physicists, many of them refugees or expatriates, gathered
together in a strange self-contained community.

In simple diagrammatic form the whole effort looked something
like that shown in Figure 1 on p. 18.

The research work of the project was mostly carried out on contract
in university laboratories. Construction and operation of the plants was
undertaken by industry. The Army's so-called 'Manhattan District'
under General L. R. Groves acted as entrepreneur and co-ordinated
and controlled the huge complex program. To give an idea of the scale,
when it was handed over to the United States Atomic Energy Commission in 1946 the project comprised 37 installations in 19 states and
in Canada; had about 37 800 contractor employees; and represented a
wartime investment of more than $2.2 billion.


## Political/moral problems about the bomb

There were three such problems. Should the bomb be made? What
attempts could be made during the war to forestall a possible nuclear
arms race — in particular, should Russia* be told about the bomb
work? Was it necessary to use the bomb against the Japanese?

No politician or scientist is recorded as having doubts on the first
question in view of the intense fear that Germany might develop a
bomb first. By the time Germany had surrendered in May 1945 the
bombs were nearly ready. It was then discovered that Germany, after a
good start, was nowhere near producing an atomic bomb.

Some scientists were very concerned with postwar international
control of atomic weapons. A group of scientists at Chicago in which
Szilard was prominent produced a famous memorandum which
concentrated largely on the use of the bomb (see next para.). Niels
Bohr, one of the scientific giants of the century, was preoccupied with
attitudes to Russia. When the Allies brought him out of occupied
Denmark in 1943 and he was told about the atomic bomb, he immediately realized that this unparalleled weapon must bring fundamental
change to the world. He saw that postwar life would be dominated by
tension between Russia and the West, and that the only chance of
forestalling a nuclear arms race between the two sides was to tell
Russia about the bomb before it had been used, and to attempt to
agree on control before there was any apparent threat of duress. He

* Russia had been an ally of USA and Britain since June 1941 when she had been
  invaded by Germany.

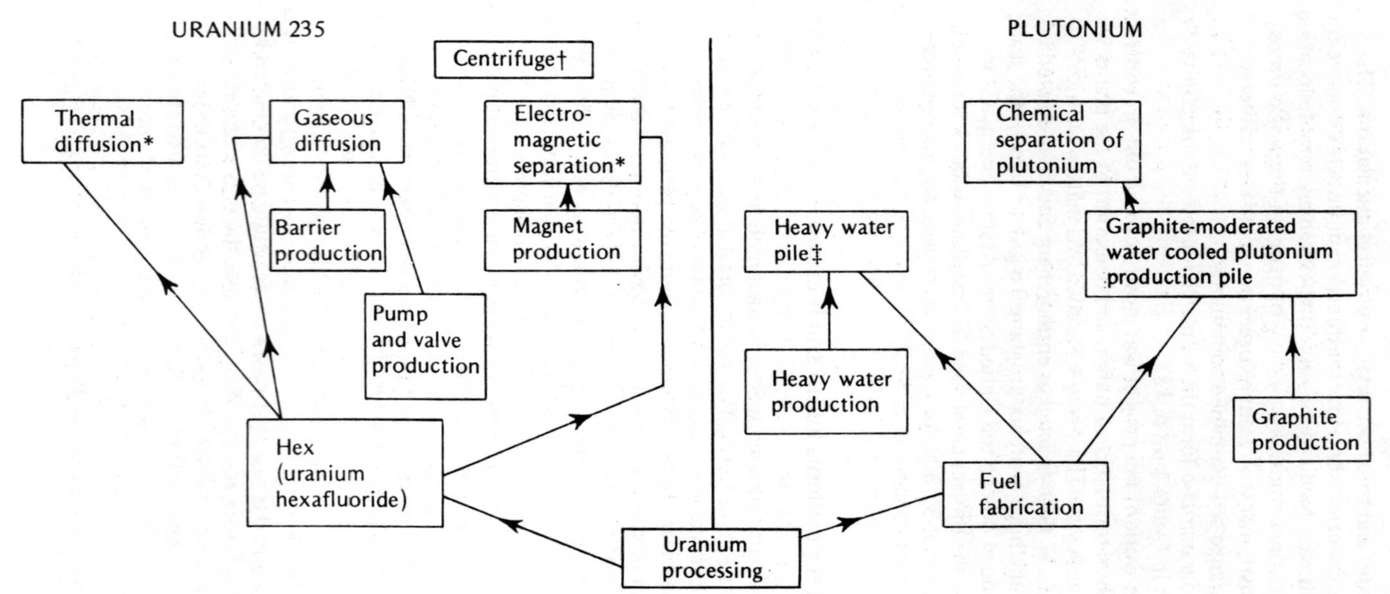



* Ceased September 1945.

† Investigated but not used for production.

‡ Not used for production in W W II.

**Figure 1   Bomb design and production**

tirelessly advocated this with Churchill and Roosevelt. But they, desperately worried about Russian behavior in Europe, signed an agreement that they would not disclose 'the secret' and added a clause that implied that Bohr might be a Russian spy. See Gowing (1964), pp. 346–366. Sherwin (1975), pp. 90–114, also deals with this.

Misconceptions have grown up about the decision to use the bomb against the Japanese. *First*, that it was done with very little thought: in fact there was much discussion and heart-searching in the United States, though not in Britain which was simply asked to agree. *Second*, that the bombs were dropped to justify the vast expenditure on the project and/or to forestall Russia's entry into the Japanese war. While some of those in the project did want 'their' bomb to end the war, and while neither the US nor Britain by the summer of 1945 wanted Russia's entry, these do not seem to have been prime causes for the release of the bombs. The bombs were dropped primarily to end the Japanese war as soon as possible. *Third*, that no warning was given to Japan. The Potsdam declaration, calling on Japan to make peace or suffer complete and utter destruction, was made less than two weeks before the first atomic bomb was dropped. It did not mention the bomb but departed from the earlier doctrine of unconditional surrender. *Fourth*, that the bombs were dropped in the face of the opposition of the atomic scientists. But the American committee of seven under the Secretary of War, set up to consider the matter, included three eminent scientists and had a distinguished scientific advisory panel*. They discussed whether the Japanese should be given a striking, harmless demonstration of the bombs before military use, but believed this to be impracticable. When the Chicago Group's memorandum was followed by a poll of the scientists at the Chicago Laboratory, over 60% of the scientists favoured a military demonstration; the percentage at other laboratories if polled would probably have been higher. In fact when the bombs fell, terrible though they were, they caused fewer casualties than some 'conventional' bombing attacks.

For the use of the bomb see the summary in Gowing (1964), chapter 14; Hewlett and Anderson (1962), chapter 11, and Sherwin (1975), chapter 8. See also Barnaby (1977).


## The German project

The crucial discovery of uranium fission at the end of 1938 had been made in Germany and, although many of the best nuclear scientists had left Germany, 16 or so very eminent ones were left including

---

* When the scientific advisory panel reported they had added a significant disclaimer: 'we have no claim to special competence in solving the political, social and military problems which are presented by the advent of atomic power'.

Heisenberg, von Laue, Hahn, Strassmann, and von Weizsäcker. Once
Peierls and Frisch had written their memorandum their conclusions
seemed such an obvious deduction from published work that no-one
could believe that the Germans would not follow the same lines. This
was the strong spur to the British and US projects.

Until 1942 German and Allied atomic research covered much the
same ground but then Germany fell behind. Although Germany's
scientists had grasped the basic theoretical concepts — Gowing (1964),
pp. 367—368, is wrong on this — her effort was like the early US effort;
her scientists, unlike the Maud Committee, could not work together
and fit all the different pieces of the puzzle into the complete jigsaw.
If their work had been as complete as Irving (1967) suggests, the leading
German scientists interned in a house near Cambridge would not have
been so incredulous when they heard the news of the atomic bomb
dropped on Hiroshima.

Other shortcomings of the German project suggested by Irving are
the inability of scientific groups to work together, especially the pure
and applied physicists; some mistakes in experimental physics; lack of
government support for a large-scale project; a gulf between science and
industry; shortage of materials such as heavy water*. Allied intelligence
relating to the German effort proved uncannily accurate but up to
the end it was not safe to assume the Germans had made so little
progress. It has sometimes been suggested that the Germans pursued an
atomic bomb unenthusiastically because of moral scruples. (e.g. Jungk
(1970), chapter VI, section VII and Irving (1962), pp. 268.) This is
quite unwarranted. It was easy to say this afterwards but there is no
impartial contemporary evidence to this effect.


## The Russian project

On hearing of the Hahn—Strassmann fission experiment at the end of
1938, a leading Soviet physicist† is reported to have said 'Do you know
what this new discovery means? It means that a bomb can be built
that will destroy a city out to a radius of maybe 10 kilometres'. (York,
1976, p. 29). Research work of high quality but on a very small scale
began but the Nazi invasion in June 1941 brought it to a halt.

Peter Kapitza (who had worked with Rutherford at Cambridge) told
a scientific conference in Moscow in 1941 that even a small atom bomb,
if it could be realized, could easily annihilate a great capital city, and
another eminent physicist warned the Societ Defense Committee in
May 1942 that an atomic bomb must be made without delay. In

* The Germans, having measured the cross-section of graphite, wrongly believed
the only possible moderator for a reactor was heavy water (Weart, 1977). The
Allies ensured, through operations of great bravery, that supplies of heavy
water were denied to Germany.

† Igor Tamm.

February 1943 after the invasion had been stemmed, a modest atomic program began, under the physicist, Igor Kurchatov.

Britain and the US officially gave no information to the USSR about the Manhattan project during the war but spies passed on detailed information. The official US report of the Manhattan project *Atomic Energy* (Smyth, 1945), called the Smyth Report, published only a few days after the atomic bombs fell, gave valuable guidance on methods of producing fissile material and was very widely read in Russia. Soviet research began to accelerate.

## Reading

ESSENTIAL

*British project*
Gowing (1964), passim.

*US project*
Hewlett and Anderson (1962), pp. 116–407.

*Political questions*
Gowing (1964), chapter 14, pp. 85–89.
Hewlett and Anderson (1962), chapter 11.

*German project*
Irving (1967).
Goudsmit (1947).
Groves (1962).

*Russian project*
Kramish (1959).
Modelski (1959), chapters 2 and 3.
York (1976), pp. 29–41.

*Japanese project*
Weiner (1978).

ADDITIONAL

*British project*
Clark (1961).
Pierre (1972).

*Manhattan Project*
Groueff (1967).
Groves (1962).
Strauss (1962).

*Political questions*
Sherwin (1975).
Jungk (1970).
Truman (1955), chapter XXI.

**Points for discussion or essays**

1. Knowledge about atomic fission was publicly available to all at the outbreak of war. Why then was the Peierls—Frisch memorandum so important? What does this suggest about the way scientists handle knowledge?
2. Why was the Maud Report so important?
3. Discuss the changing balance of power between Britain and the US as it was reflected in the wartime atomic project.
4. Why did the Germans fail to produce an atomic bomb?
5. What was the importance of foreign scientists (including British and refugee scientists) to, and in, the US bomb program?
6. What were the factors that made USA the only country that produced an atomic bomb during the war?
7. Why did some scientists (e.g. Szilard) urge the development of atomic bombs in 1939 and argue against their use in 1945?
8. How far could atomic scientists see the consequences of their wartime work?
9. Do you think it would have been better or worse for mankind if the atomic bombs had not been (a) developed (b) used in the Second World War?
10. What made the atomic bomb so different from conventional weapons?

# Chapter Four
# The Atomic Bomb
# and the Postwar World, 1945-53

Even in this short period of eight years there is so much material and
so many areas to be investigated that the topic has been confined to
four main points:
1. International control and disarmament.
2. Atomic relations between the Western powers.
3. Development of the projects of the atomic powers.
4. The political role of the scientists.

## International control and disarmament

At the end of the war politicians, scientists and the public alike believed
passionately that without international control of atomic energy the
human race might perish. A United Nations Commission was set up to
make specific proposals for international control, and was preceded by
a brilliant American report which explored all the technical and
scientific problems and proposed an organization which would solve
them.

The plan, coming at the very early stage of development, was probably
not only the first but the last real opportunity for control. But it never
stood a chance. The lesson of the League of Nations between the two
World Wars was painfully relearned: any weapon control system,
however scientifically plausible, was impossible unless mutual trust
existed between the leading powers. Since such trust did not exist
each world power felt obliged to look after its own interests and make
itself as strong as possible in nuclear weapons.

The USA was the sole nuclear power and was anxious to remain so.
The USSR could not permit a situation where America possessed atomic
bombs while she did not. Mr. Attlee, the new British Prime Minister,
wrote with emotion 'The new world order must start now', but at the
same time was intent on making Britain's own atomic position as strong
as possible.

In 1948 the United Nations Atomic Energy Commission finally died
of debility (summary in Gowing, 1974, Vol 1, pp. 87–92). From the
end of 1947 the cold war between East and West was in full swing, and
although the atomic bomb intensified the fear and iciness of the cold
war it probably did much to prevent it from becoming a fighting war.

The scientists in all three countries broadly endorsed their governments' views and weapon policies in the late 1940s. Even Einstein in
the early postwar years insisted that the US should maintain control of
the bomb until the world government he advocated was ready to

function. Bertrand Russell, later a passionate nuclear disarmer, was an
equally passionate advocate of preventive war as late as 1948 (Clark,
1975, pp. 523, 528). It is not true that a strong nuclear disarmament
movement began immediately after the war. The British Campaign for
Nuclear Disarmament did not begin until 1957, 12 years after the war
ended.

## Atomic relations between the Western powers

The atomic bomb deepened the rifts between East and West and also,
paradoxically, between the Western allies. The Manhattan Project had
developed out of the work of scientists in Britain, and in the last two
years of the war there was a close Anglo-American atomic partnership
with Britain as junior partner. The British believed — and Roosevelt
had promised — that this partnership would continue after the war.
But in 1946, with no regard for their commitments, the USA passed
the McMahon Act, which prevented effective atomic co-operation not
only with potential enemies but even between America and Britain.
There was a belief that there existed a secret of the bomb and its
associated technology; that this was essential to the safety of the state;
that America alone possessed it and that it could be kept inviolate. This
belief fostered McCarthyism and hysteria in the US. Even when the US
and Britain were very close military partners again in the late 1940s and
1950s, atomic energy was excluded from the partnership until 1955.
The British ceaselessly tried to persuade the Americans to renew atomic
collaboration, but with little success for many years.

Collaboration remained strong only in the procurement of uranium,
where the British could help the Americans (Gowing, 1974, Vol 1,
chapters 3, 4, 8, 9, 11, 12; Hewlett and Anderson, 1962, pp. 285–92;
Hewlett and Duncan, 1969, passim). American reluctance was the
greater because of the atomic spy cases, of which the most dramatic
was that of Fuchs, a German refugee to Britain who worked at Los
Alamos in the war and told the Russians everything he knew (Moorehead, 1952; Gowing, 1974, Vol 2, chapter 16).

Because of her fear of alienating the United States, Britain turned
her back on the atomic collaboration which France desired and could
not co-operate with any of the Commonwealth countries except
Canada (Gowing, 1974, Vol 1, chapters 5 and 10).

## Development of the projects of the atomic powers

### THE UNITED STATES PROJECT

It has sometimes been suggested that the United States' decision to
drop the atomic bomb on Japan was the first move in the cold war
against Russia. This is not consistent with the rundown of the US

atomic project in the 18 months or so after the war. By the end of 1947, Los Alamos, for example, had only 12 theoretical physicists on the staff (York, 1974, p. 18). Thereafter the US project re-expanded fast. There were three military objectives:

1. A great increase in the output of atomic weapons and the development of many different and more sophisticated types of atomic weapons, including improved fission bombs as well as hydrogen bombs. By 1949 the US were making atomic weapons on a factory production scale, and carrying out a program of weapon tests (Hewlett and Duncan, 1969, chapter 6; York, 1976, pp. 15–28).
2. A program of nuclear-powered submarines, which had interested the Navy from 1939 — established as a US Atomic Energy Commission project in 1948, and pushed to a successful conclusion by Admiral Rickover (Hewlett and Duncan, 1969, pp. 206–220, 515 and passim).
3. Research into, and from 1950 development of, the hydrogen bomb (which was also called the super). This is discussed below.

These programs required a large increase in the production of fissile material, both plutonium and U235. There was at the same time the beginnings of a nuclear power programme.

The US project is described at great length and in great detail in Hewlett and Anderson (1962), and Hewlett and Duncan (1969). York's *The Advisors* (1976), is short and essential reading.


THE RUSSIAN POSTWAR PROGRAM

The Russian atomic energy project under the physicist Igor Kurchatov* developed very rapidly after the war and in August 1949 the first Soviet atom bomb test (Joe 1) was detected by US and British monitoring systems. As Fuchs confessed a few weeks later that he had given so much information to the Russians it was believed that their success was due to spies. Because Russian scientific and technological ability was underestimated the bomb was a great shock to the Americans, and even more to the British, who had expected to be the second nuclear power but whose own first bomb test was still three years away. Yet a majority of the estimates made at the end of the war, particularly from those familiar with the subject, said that it would take the Russians 'about five years' (Gowing, 1974, Vol 1, pp. 221–222).

The Russians proceeded to mass-produce atomic bombs and to develop a super. The Russian project is broadly dealt with by Kramish (1959) and Modelski (1959). Again York (1976) is strongly recommended.

* Two Russian biographies have been published of Kurchatov, the Russian scientist who headed the Soviet atomic energy project (for details see York, 1976, p. 161).

Britain had no doubt at the end of the war that she should have a
native atomic project as soon as possible. At first this meant a program
for producing fissile material which might lead either to nuclear power
or nuclear weapons.* A decision to make a bomb was not taken until
the beginning of 1947 and then in the greatest possible secrecy; this
decision-making process sheds much light on the working of British
government (Gowing 1974, Vol 1, pp. 179–185).

Why was Britain so anxious to have her own atomic bomb?

1. Because having 'invented' it she felt she had a proprietorial right to
   it.
2. Strategic reasons: there seemed no defence against atomic bombs
   except possession of a deterrent.
3. Belief in Britain's great power status.
4. Britain's relationship with the US. In atomic affairs the US treated
   Britain badly after the war (see above) and Britain refused to be
   bullied out of atomic energy by them.

The United Kingdom project was, by British standards, brilliantly
successful as a large-scale scientific and engineering enterprise working
on the furthest frontiers of knowledge. The project cost relatively little
in terms of resources; the complex of industrial plants was built to time
and to cost; all of them worked well. However Britain could not keep
pace with the nuclear weapon projects of the two super powers. Her
first primitive Nagasaki-type atomic bomb was exploded in the Monte
Bello Islands near Australia in October 1952. Thus Britain was three
years behind USSR in testing an atomic bomb; in the subsequent
H-bomb race she was to be four years behind.

Britain's nuclear power program developed out of her weapon
project. Calder Hall in Cumbria, opened in 1956 as the world's first
industrial scale nuclear power station, was built absolutely to schedule
and has worked faultlessly for over 20 years. It was planned in 1952 as
a dual-purpose station whose principal function was to produce additional plutonium for the weapons programme. Note that Britain did not
have a nuclear submarine project in this period — a fact which affected
the type of reactor development.

Gowing (1974) deals in great detail with the British program. Volume 1
deals with policy making and international relations and Volume 2
with the execution of policy: for example, the scientific and engineering
programs and methods, nuclear power, the cost, health and safety, the
first bomb. Both volumes have very full indexes, so that readers should
be able to pick out the subject matter that interests them. Pierre (1972),
pp. 67–151, gives a very good and readable account of Britain's nuclear
weapon policies.

* This course does not attempt to deal with delivery systems, but see Gowing
  (1974), Vol 1, pp. 209, 234–5.

France was the fourth nuclear power. French scientists had been the first in 1939 to report the possibility of a chain reaction in uranium and several of them had worked in the British and Canadian project during the war. They built up a postwar project in France which was small at first but produced plutonium bombs by 1960 and hydrogen bombs by 1968 (Goldschmidt, 1967, Scheinman, 1965, Part II, and Moss, 1970, pp. 322–333).

China was the fifth atomic power. She began to develop a nuclear capability in 1950 and exploded her first atomic bomb (a U235 bomb) in 1964 and her first hydrogen bomb in 1967 (Moss, 1970, pp. 333–343).

## The political role of the scientists

Atomic scientists did not play a major political role in postwar Britain and for the most part simply co-operated with the government. The only exceptions are Patrick Blackett, the Nobel laureate, who wrote important memoranda to the British government on nuclear weapons policy (Gowing, 1974, Vol 1, pp. 194–206) and a widely read book;* the two physicists who gave information to the Russians and the one physicist who fled to Russia (Gowing, 1974, Vol 2, chapter 16).

In the postwar United States the atomic scientists, more especially the physicists, came to the front of the political stage. Indeed the bomb had elevated their profession in the eyes of the public to a level inhabited in a previous generation by the priesthood (Greenberg, 1969). The American scientists had one immediate postwar goal: they were determined to see civilian, not military control of the US atomic project, and in this they were triumphantly successful. They formed one of the most effective pressure groups Washington had ever seen. They ensured that one congressional bill was dropped and replaced by an Act that gave them what they wanted: this was the same McMahon Act that prevented dissemination of technical information about atomic energy to other countries (Smith, 1965, chapter 13).

Thereafter the American atomic scientists, like the British scientists, worked closely with their governments in the development of atomic weapons, because they believed in the reality of the cold war and feared Russian intentions. However in 1950 there was the beginning of the end of the symbiosis between scientists and government and of the solidarity

* Blackett (1948), *Military and Political Consequences of Atomic Energy*, Turnstile Press.

and unity of the scientists themselves. The main occasion for this was the US debate whether or not to develop a hydrogen bomb. It was clear that this would be a transformation in warfare, in no sense at all comparable with conventional weapons. Its destructive power would amount to genocide.

Two questions arose about the hydrogen bomb. First whether it was scientifically and technically possible and secondly, if the first answer was yes, whether the US should for political and moral reasons go ahead. One group of scientists felt passionately that if enough resources were poured into the project a hydrogen bomb could be made, and that in view of the Communist threat it must be made. The scientific advisory panel of the Atomic Energy Commission opposed this view. They believed that with a concentrated effort a weapon probably could be produced, but that the weapon would be an intolerable threat to the future of the human race and should not be developed. They were convinced that the US superiority in atomic weapons was so great that renunciation of this development, in the hope that Russia would follow suit, would not imperil American security.

The scientific advisory committee no longer retreated from big political questions as they had done in 1945 when asked about the use of the atomic bomb on Japan. York (1976), which is indispensable reading, reconsiders this report and shows how wise and realistic it was in the light of the weapon tests of the 1950s.

President Truman decided that the US should develop the hydrogen bomb and thereafter the scientists on the advisory panel did everything they could to hasten this work. This was partly because of the outbreak of the Korean War and partly because the project looked much more promising technically. But even though the ranks of the American scientists seemed to have closed around the H-bomb, and even though their understanding seemed once more complete, the bitter disagreements of this time left deep rifts that were not bridged. The chairman of the scientific advisory panel which had opposed the H-bomb had been Robert Oppenheimer, the wartime director of Los Alamos, and in 1954 the government decided to withdraw his security clearance. Long quasi-judicial hearings were held, and the transcript is the best view we have of the atomic scientists' behavior, of their differences of view and soul-searching. York (1976) is again indispensable. For those who have the time see USAEC Hearings (1971), Major (1971) and Stern (1971).

The atomic bomb had indeed plunged scientists up to their necks in politics, that is in an ocean hitherto unfamiliar to them. It is perhaps worth concluding by saying that, although they showed considerable foresight about nuclear weapons, almost nothing was said about the problems of creating dangerous radioactive materials such as plutonium with its half-life of 24 000 years.

# Reading

ESSENTIAL

Gowing (1974).
Hewlett and Anderson (1962).  } Select reading according to interests
Hewlett and Duncan (1969).    } by chapter headings and index
Hewlett (1974).
Moss (1970).
Pierre (1972), pp. 68–144.
York (1976).


ADDITIONAL

Clark (1975), passim.
Goldschmidt (1962), chapters 3 to 8.
Goldschmidt (1967), pp. 113–292.
Goldsmith (1976), chapters 8, 9, 11.
Greenberg (1969).
Kramish (1959).
Modelski (1959).
Moorehead (1952).
Major (1971).
Scheinman (1965).
Smith (1965).
Stern (1971).
USAEC Oppenheimer Hearings (1971).

---

## Points for discussion or essays

1. Why was the US anxious to retain an atomic monopoly after the war?
2. Was Britain right to develop her own atomic bomb? Did she have any alternative?
3. Was Britain justified in her claim to an equal atomic partnership with US after the war? How did this claim affect her relationships with other countries?
4. Did Britain's wartime atomic work affect her postwar power status?
5. Why were Britain and the US so shocked by the first Russian test in August 1949?
6. Discuss the significance of the atomic spies.
7. Why was the British atomic project of 1945–52 an industrial success?
8. Discuss the postwar role of the atomic scientists, perhaps with special reference to Robert Oppenheimer.

# Appendix One
# The Idea of a Chain Reaction

## (Extract from reminiscences of Leo Szilard)

. . . In 1932 while I was still in Berlin, I read a book by H. G. Wells.
It was called *The World Set Free.** This book was written in 1913, one
year before the World War, and in it H. G. Wells describes the discovery
of artificial radioactivity and puts it in the year of 1933, the year in
which it actually occurred. He then proceeds to describe the liberation
of atomic energy on a large scale for industrial purposes, the development of atomic bombs, and a world war which was apparently fought
by allies of England, France, and perhaps including America, against
Germany and Austria, the powers located in the central part of Europe.
He places this war in the year 1956, and in this war the major cities of
the world are all destroyed by atomic bombs. Up to this point the book
is exceedingly vivid and realistic. From then on the book gets to be a
little, shall I say, utopian. With the world in shambles, a conference is
called in Brissago in Italy, in which a world government is set up.

This book made a very great impression on me, but I didn't regard
it as anything *but* fiction. It didn't start me thinking whether or not
such things could in fact happen. I had not been working in nuclear
physics up to that time.

Now, this really doesn't belong here, but I will nevertheless tell you
of a curious conversation which I had, also in 1932, in Berlin. The
conversation was with a very interesting man named Otto Mandl, who
was an Austrian, and who became a wealthy timber merchant in
England, and whose main claim to fame was that he had discovered
H. G. Wells at a time when none of his works had been translated into
German. He went to H. G. Wells and acquired the exclusive right to
publish his works in German, and this is how H. G. Wells became
known on the Continent. In 1932 something went wrong with his
timber business in London, and he found himself again in Berlin. I had
met him previously in London and I met him again in Berlin and there
ensued a memorable conversation. Otto Mandl said he not only thought,
he *knew* what it would take to save mankind from a series of ever-
recurring wars that could destroy it. He said that man has a heroic
streak in himself. Man is not satisfied with a happy idyllic life. He has
a need to fight and to encounter danger. And he concluded that what
mankind must do to save itself is to launch an enterprise aimed at
leaving the earth. On this start he thought the energies of mankind
could be concentrated and the need for heroism could be satisfied.

* Wells (1914), *The World Set Free: A Story of Mankind*, London.

I remember my own reaction very well. I told him that this was somewhat new to me, and that I really didn't know whether I would agree
with him. The only thing I could say was this: that if I came to the
conclusion that this was what mankind needed, and if I wanted to
contribute something to save mankind, then I would probably go into
nuclear physics, because only through the liberation of atomic energy
could we obtain the means which would enable man not only to leave
the earth but to leave the solar system.

I was not thinking any more about this conversation or about
H. G. Wells's books either, until I found myself in London about the
time of the British Association meeting in September 1933. I read in
the newspapers a speech by Lord Rutherford, who was quoted as
saying that he who talks about the liberation of atomic energy on an
industrial basis is talking moonshine. This set me pondering as I was
walking the streets of London, and I remember that I stopped for a
red light at the intersection of Southampton Row. As the light changed
to green and I crossed the street, it suddenly occurred to me that if we
could find an element which is split by neutrons and which would emit
*two* neutrons when it absorbed *one* neutron, such an element, if
assembled in sufficiently large mass, could sustain a nuclear chain
reaction. I didn't see at the moment just how one would go about
finding such an element, or what experiments would be needed, but the
idea never left me. Soon thereafter, when the discovery of artificial
radioactivity by Joliot and Mme. Joliot was announced, I suddenly
saw that tools were at hand to explore the possibility of such a chain
reaction. I talked to a number of people about this. I remember that I
mentioned it to G. P. Thomson* and to Blackett,† but I couldn't
evoke any enthusiasm.

I had one candidate for an element which might be instable [sic] in the
sense of splitting off neutrons when it disintegrates, and that was
beryllium . . . As it turned out later beryllium cannot sustain a chain
reaction and is, in fact, stable . . .

When I gave up beryllium I did not give up the thought that there
might be another element which could sustain a chain reaction. And in
the spring of 1934 I had applied for a patent which described the laws
governing such a chain reaction. It was the first time, I think, that the
concept of critical mass was developed and that a chain reaction was
seriously discussed. Knowing what this would mean — and I knew it
because I had read H. G. Wells — I did not want this patent to become
public. The only way to keep it from becoming public was to assign it
to the government. So I assigned this patent to the British Admiralty . . .

* George Paget Thomson (son of J. J. Thomson), in 1933, professor of physics
   at University of London.
† P. M. S. Blackett; in 1933 professor of physics at University of London.

*Note* This extract is reproduced from Fleming & Bailyn (1969) *The Intellectual
Migration*, Harvard Univeristy Press, pp. 99—102.

# Appendix Two
# Szilard, Rabi, and Fermi
# Discuss Uranium Fission

**(Extract from reminiscences of Leo Szilard)**

. . . Wigner told me of Hahn's discovery: Hahn found that uranium breaks into two parts when it absorbs the neutron and this is the process which we call fission. When I heard this I saw immediately that these fragments, being heavier than corresponds to their charge, must emit neutrons; and if enough neutrons are emitted in this fission process, then it should be, of course, possible to sustain a chain reaction; all the things which H. G. Wells had predicted appeared suddenly real to me.

At that time it was already clear, not only to me but to many other people . . . that we were at the threshold of another world war. And so it became, it seemed to us, urgent to set up experiments which would show whether, in fact, neutrons are emitted in the fission process of uranium. I thought that if neutrons are in fact emitted in fission, this should be kept secret from the Germans; so I was very eager to contact Joliot and Fermi, the two men who were most likely to think of this possibility. I was still in Princeton and staying at Wigner's apartment . . . But I was laid up with fever for about a week or ten days. In the meantime, Fermi had also thought of the possibility of a neutron emission and the possibility of a chain reaction and he went to a private meeting in Washington and talked about these things. Since it was a private meeting, the cat was not entirely out of the bag, but its tail was sticking out. When I recovered I went to see Rabi and Rabi told me that Fermi had similar ideas and that he had talked about them in Washington. Fermi was not in, so I told Rabi to please talk to Fermi and say that these things ought to be kept secret because it was very likely that neutrons are emitted, that this might lead to a chain reaction, and this might lead to the construction of bombs. So Rabi said he would, and I went back home to bed at the Kings Crown Hotel.

A few days later I got up to see Rabi and asked, "Did you talk to Fermi?" Rabi said, "Yes, I did." I said, "What did Fermi say?" and he said Fermi said, 'Nuts!' So I said, "Why did he say, 'Nuts!'?" and Rabi said, "Well, I don't know, but he is in and we can ask him." So we went over the Fermil's office, and Rabi said to Fermi, "Look, Fermi, I told you what Szilard thought and you said, 'Nuts!' and Szilard wants to know why you said, 'Nuts!' So Fermi said, "Well, there is the *remote* possibility that neutrons may be emitted in the fission of uranium and then of course that a chain reaction can be made." Rabi said, "What do you mean by 'remote possibility'?" and Fermi said, "Well, 10 per cent." and Rabi said, "Ten per cent is not a remote possibility if it means that we may die of it. If I have pneumonia and the doctor tells me that there is a remote possibility that I might die, and that it's 10 per cent, I get excited about it."

*Note* This extract is taken from Fleming and Bailyn (1969), op cit, pp. 106—107.

# Appendix Three
# Memorandum on the Properties of a Radioactive Super - bomb

## by O. R. Frisch and R. Peierls

The attached detailed report* concerns the possibility of constructing a 'super-bomb' which utilizes the energy stored in atomic nuclei as a source of energy. The energy liberated in the explosion of such a super-bomb is about the same as that produced by the explosion of 1000 tons of dynamite. This energy is liberated in a small volume, in which it will, for an instant, produce a temperature comparable to that in the interior of the sun. The blast from such an explosion would destroy life in a wide area. The size of this area is difficult to estimate, but it will probably cover the centre of a big city.

In addition, some part of the energy set free by the bomb goes to produce radioactive substances, and these will emit very powerful and dangerous radiations. The effect of these radiations is greatest immediately after the explosion, but it decays only gradually and even for days after the explosion any person entering the affected area will be killed.

Some of this radioactivity will be carried along with the wind and will spread the contamination; several miles downwind this may kill people.

In order to produce such a bomb it is necessary to treat a few hundred pounds of uranium by a process which will separate from the uranium its light isotope (U235) of which it contains about 0.7%. Methods for the separation of isotopes have recently been developed. They are slow and they have not until now been applied to uranium, whose chemical properties give rise to technical difficulties. But these difficulties are by no means insuperable. We have not sufficient experience with large-scale chemical plant to give a reliable estimate of the cost, but it is certainly not prohibitive.

It is a property of these super-bombs that there exists a 'critical size' of about one pound. A quantity of separated uranium isotope that exceeds the critical amount is explosive; yet a quantity less than the critical amount is absolutely safe. The bomb would therefore be manufactured in two (or more) parts, each being less than the critical size, and in transport all danger of a premature explosion would be avoided if these parts were kept at a distance of a few inches from each other.

* This can be found in Gowing (1964), *Britain and Atomic Energy 1939–1945*, Macmillan, pp. 389–393.

The bomb would be provided with a mechanism that brings the two parts together when the bomb is intended to go off. Once the parts are joined to form a block which exceeds the critical amount, the effect of the penetrating radiation always present in the atmosphere will initiate the explosion within a second or so.

The mechanism which brings the parts of the bomb together must be arranged to work fairly rapidly because of the possibility of the bomb exploding when the critical conditions have only just been reached. In this case the explosion will be far less powerful. It is never possible to exclude this altogether, but one can easily ensure that only, say, one bomb out of 100 will fail in this way, and since in any case the explosion is strong enough to destroy the bomb itself, this point is not serious.

We do not feel competent to discuss the strategic value of such a bomb, but the following conclusions seem certain:

1. As a weapon, the super-bomb would be practically irresistible. There is no material or structure that could be expected to resist the force of the explosion. If one thinks of using the bomb for breaking through a line of fortifications, it should be kept in mind that the radioactive radiations will prevent anyone from approaching the affected territory for several days; they will equally prevent defenders from reoccupying the affected positions. The advantage would lie from the side which can determine most accurately just when it is safe to re-enter the area; this is likely to be the aggressor, who knows the location of the bomb in advance.
2. Owing to the spreading of radioactive substances with the wind, the bomb could probably not be used without killing large numbers of civilians, and this may make it unsuitable as a weapon for use by this country. (Use as a depth charge near a naval base suggests itself, but even there it is likely that it would cause great loss of civilian life by flooding and by the radioactive radiations.)
3. We have no information that the same idea has also occurred to other scientists but since all the theoretical data bearing on this problem are published, it is quite conceivable that Germany is, in fact, developing this weapon. Whether this is the case is difficult to find out, since the plant for the separation of isotopes need not be of such a size as to attract attention. Information that could be helpful in this respect would be data about the exploitation of the uranium mines under German control (mainly in Czechoslovakia) and about any recent German purchases of uranium abroad. It is likely that the plant would be controlled by Dr. K. Clusius (Professor of Physical Chemistry in Munich University), the inventor of the best method for separating isotopes, and therefore information as to his whereabouts and status might also give an important clue.

At the same time it is quite possible that nobody in Germany has yet realized that the separation of the uranium isotopes would make the construction of a super-bomb possible. Hence it is of extreme importance to keep this report secret since any rumour about the connection between uranium separation and a super-bomb may set German scientists thinking along the right lines.

4. If one works on the assumption that Germany is, or will be, in the possession of this weapon, it must be realized that no shelters are available that would be effective and could be used on a large scale. The most effective reply would be a counter-threat with a similar bomb. Therefore it seems to us important to start production as soon and as rapidly as possible, even if it is not intended to use the bomb as a means of attack. Since the separation of the necessary amount of uranium is, in the most favourable circumstances, a matter of several months, it would obviously be too late to start production when such a bomb is known to be in the hands of Germany, and the matter seems, therefore, very urgent.

5. As a measure of precaution, it is important to have detection squads available in order to deal with the radioactive effects of such a bomb. Their task would be to approach the danger zone with measuring instruments, to determine the extent and probable duration of the danger and to prevent people from entering the danger zone. This is vital since the radiations kill instantly only in very strong doses whereas weaker doses produce delayed effects and hence near the edges of the danger zone people would have no warning until it were too late.

For their own protection, the detection squads would enter the danger zone in motor-cars or aeroplanes which are armoured with lead plates, which absorb most of the dangerous radiation. The cabin would have to be hermetically sealed and oxygen carried in cylinders because of the danger from contaminated air.

The detection staff would have to know exactly the greatest dose of radiation to which a human being can be exposed safely for a short time. This safety limit is not at present known with sufficient accuracy and further biological research for this purpose is urgently required.

As regards the reliability of the conclusions outlined above, it may be said that they are not based on direct experiments, since nobody has ever yet built a super-bomb, but they are mostly based on facts, which by recent research in nuclear physics, have been very safely established. The only uncertainty concerns the critical size for the bomb. We are fairly confident that the critical size is roughly a pound or so, but for this estimate we have to rely on certain theoretical ideas which have not been positively confirmed. If the critical size were appreciably larger than we believe it to be, the technical difficulties in the way of constructing the bomb would be enhanced. The point can be definitely settled as soon as a small amount of uranium has been separated, and we think in view of the importance of the matter immediate steps should be taken to reach at least this stage; meanwhile it is also possible to carry out certain experiments which, while they cannot settle the question with absolute finality, could, if their result were positive, give strong support to our conclusions.

*Note* This memorandum is reproduced from R. W. Clark (1965), *Tizard*, Methuen, pp. 215–217. Clark says (p. 214) "No copy exists in the official archives, nor have the authors retained one, a fact which accounts for the absence of any reference to it in the official history of Britain's Atomic Energy Project *'Britain and Atomic Energy, 1939–1945'*, Margaret Gowing."

# Appendix Four
# A Warning to President Roosevelt

**Letter of transmittal from Leo Szilard to Dr. Alexander Sachs: 15 August 1939**

Dear Dr. Sachs:

Enclosed I am sending you a letter from Prof. Albert Einstein, which is addressed to President Roosevelt and which he sent to me with the request of forwarding it through such channels as might appear appropriate. If you see your way to bring this letter to the attention of the President, I am certain Prof. Einstein would appreciate your doing so; otherwise would you be good enough to return the letter to me?

If a man, having courage and imagination, could be found and if such a man were put — in accordance with Dr. Einstein's suggestion — in the position to act with some measure of authority in this matter, this would certainly be an important step forward. In order that you may be able to see of what assistance such a man could be in our work, allow me please to give you a short account of the past history of the case.

In January this year, when I realized that there was a remote possibility of setting up a chain reaction in a large mass of uranium, I communicated with Prof. E. P. Wigner of Princeton University and Prof. E. Teller of George Washington University, Washington, D.C., and the three of us remained in constant consultation ever since. First of all it appeared necessary to perform certain fundamental experiments for which the use of about one gram of radium was required. Since at that time we had no certainty and had to act on a remote possibility, we could hardly hope to succeed in persuading a university laboratory to take charge of these experiments, or even to acquire the radium needed. Attempts to obtain the necessary funds from other sources appeared to be equally hopeless. In these circumstances a few of us physicists formed an association, called 'Association for Scientific Collaboration', collected some funds among ourselves, rented about one gram of radium, and I arranged with the Physics Department of Columbia University for their permission to carry out the proposed experiments at Columbia. These experiments led early in March to rather striking results.

At about the same time Prof. E. Fermi, also at Columbia, made experiments of his own, independently of ours, and came to identical conclusions.

A close collaboration arose out of this coincidence, and recently Dr. Fermi and I jointly performed experiments which make it appear

probable that a chain reaction in uranium can be achieved in the
immediate future.

The path along which we have to move is now clearly defined, but it
takes some courage to embark on the journey. The experiments will be
costly since we will now have to work with tons of material rather than
– as hitherto – with kilograms. Two or possibly three different alter-
natives will have to be tried; failures, set-backs and some unavoidable
danger to human life will have to faced. We have so far made use of the
Association for Scientific Collaboration to overcome the difficulty of
persuading other organizations to take financial risks, and also to
overcome the general reluctance to take action on the basis of
probabilities in the absence of certainty. Now, in the face of greater
certainty, but also greater risks, it will become necessary either to
strengthen this association both morally and financially, or to find new
ways which would serve the same purpose. We have to approach as
quickly as possible public-spirited private persons and try to enlist
their financial co-operation, or, failing in this, we would have to try to
enlist the collaboration of the leading firms of the electrical or chemical
industry.

Other aspects of the situation have to be kept in mind. Dr. Wigner is
taking the stand that it is our duty to enlist the co-operation of the
Administration. A few weeks ago he came to New York in order to
discuss this point with Dr. Teller and me, and on his initiative conversations took place between Dr. Einstein and the three of us. This led to
Dr. Einstein's decision to write to the President.

I am enclosing a memorandum which will give you some of the views
and opinions which were expressed in these conversations.

I wish to make it clear that, in approaching you, I am acting in the
capacity of a trustee of the Association for Scientific Collaboration,
and that I have no authority to speak in the name of the Physics
Department of Columbia University, of which I am a guest.

Yours sincerely,

## Letter from Professor Albert Einstein to President Roosevelt: August 1939

Sir:

Some recent work by E. Fermi and L. Szilard, which has been
communicated to me in manuscript, leads me to expect that the
element uranium may be turned into a new and important source of
energy in the immediate future. Certain aspects of the situation seem to
call for watchfulness and, if necessary, quick action on the part of the
administration. I believe, therefore, that it is my duty to bring to your
attention the following facts and recommendations.

In the course of the last four months it has been made probable —
through the work of Joliot in France as well as Fermi and Szilard in
America — that it may become possible to set up nuclear chain reactions
in a large mass of uranium, by which vast amounts of power and large
quantities of new radium-like elements would be generated. Now it
appears almost certain that this could be achieved in the immediate
future.

This new phenomenon would also lead to the construction of bombs,
and it is conceivable — though much less certain — that extremely
powerful bombs of a new type may thus be constructed. A single bomb
of this type, carried by boat or exploded in a port, might very well
destroy the whole port together with some of the surrounding territory.
However such bombs might well prove to be too heavy for transportation by air.

The United States has only very poor ores of uranium in moderate
quantities. There is some good ore in Canada and the former Czechoslovakia, while the most important source of uranium is the Belgian
Congo.

In view of this situation you may think it desirable to have some
permanent contact maintained between the administration and the
group of physicists working on chain reaction in America. One possible
way of achieving this might be for you to entrust with this task a person
who has your confidence and who could perhaps serve in an unofficial
capacity. His task might comprise the following:

(a) To approach government departments, keep them informed of
further developments, and put forward recommendations for government action, giving particular attention to the problem of securing a
supply of uranium ore for the United States.

(b) To speed up the experimental work which is at present being
carried on within the limits of the budgets of the university laboratories,
by providing funds, if such funds be required, through his contacts
with private persons who are willing to make contributions for this
cause and perhaps also by obtaining the co-operation of industrial
laboratories which have the necessary equipment.

I understand that Germany has actually stopped the sale of uranium
from the Czechoslovakian mines which she has taken over. That she
should have taken such early action might perhaps be understood on
the ground that the son of the German Undersecretary of State, von
Weizsäcker, is attached to the Kaiser Wilhelm Institute of Berlin, where
some of the American work on uranium is now being repeated.

Yours very truly,

# Memorandum from Leo Szilard to President Roosevelt: 15 August 1939

Much experimentation on atomic disintegration was done during the past five years, but up to this year the problem of liberating nuclear energy could not be attacked with any reasonable hope for success. Early this year it became known that the element uranium can be split by neutrons. It appeared conceivable that in this nuclear process uranium itself may emit neutrons, and a few of us envisaged the possibility of liberating nuclear energy by means of a chain reaction of neutrons in uranium.

Experiments were thereupon performed, which led to striking results. One has to conclude that a nuclear chain reaction could be maintained under certain well defined conditions in a large mass of uranium. It still remains to prove this conclusion by actually setting up a chain reaction in a large-scale experiment.

This new development in physics means that a new source of power is now being created. Large amounts of energy would be liberated, and large quantities of new radioactive elements would be produced in such a chain reaction.

In medical applications of radium we have to deal with quantities of grams; the new radioactive elements could be produced in a chain reaction in quantities corresponding to tons of radium equivalents. While the practical application would include the medical field, it would not be limited to it.

A radioactive element gives a continuous release of energy for a certain period of time. The amount of energy which is released per unit weight of material may be very large, and therefore such elements might be used — if available in large quantities — as fuel for driving boats or airplanes. It should be pointed out, however, that the physiological action of the radiations emitted by these new radioactive elements makes it necessary to protect those who have to stay close to a large quantity of such an element, for instance the driver of the airplane. It may therefore be necessary to carry large quantities of lead, and this necessity might impede a development along this line, or at least limit the field of application.

Large quantities of energy would be liberated in a chain reaction, which might be utilized for purposes of power production in the form of a stationary power plant.

In view of this development it may be a question of national importance to secure an adequate supply of uranium. The United States has only very poor ores of uranium in moderate quantities; there is a good ore of uranium in Canada where the total deposit is estimated to be about 3000 tons; there may be about 1500 tons of uranium in Czechoslovakia, which is now controlled by Germany; there is an unknown amount of uranium in Russia, but the most important source of uranium, consisting of an unknown but probably very large amount of good ore, is Belgian Congo.

It is suggested therefore to explore the possibility of bringing over from Belgian Congo a large stock of pitchblend, which is the ore of both radium and uranium, and to keep this stock here for possible future use. Perhaps a large quantity of this ore might be obtained as a token reparation payment from the Belgian Government. In taking action along this line it would not be necessary officially to disclose that the uranium content of the ore is the point of interest; action might be taken on the ground that it is of value to secure a stock of the ore on account of its radium content for possible future extraction of the radium for medical purposes.

Since it is unlikely that an earnest attempt to secure a supply of uranium will be made before the possibility of a chain reaction has been visibly demonstrated, it appears necessary to do this as quickly as possible by performing a large-scale experiment. The previous experiments have prepared the ground to the extent that it is now possible clearly to define the conditions under which such a large-scale experiment would have to be carried out. Still two or three different setups may have to be tried out, or alternatively preliminary experiments have to be carried out with several tons of material if we want to decide in advance in favor of one setup or another. These experiments cannot be carried out within the limited budget which was provided for laboratory experiments in the past, and it has now become necessary either to strengthen — financially and otherwise — the organizations which concerned themselves with this work up to now, or to create some new organization for the purpose. Public-spirited private persons who are likely to be interested in supporting this enterprise should be approached without delay, or alternatively the collaboration of the chemical or the electrical industry should be sought.

The investigations were hitherto limited to chain reactions based on the action of *slow* neutrons. The neutrons emitted from the splitting uranium are fast, but they are slowed down in a mixture of uranium and a light element. Fast neutrons lose their energy in colliding with atoms of a light element in much the same way as a billiard ball loses velocity in a collision with another ball. At present it is an open question whether such a chain reaction can also be made to work with *fast* neutrons which are not slowed down.

There is reason to believe that, if fast neutrons could be used, it would be easy to construct extremely dangerous bombs. The destructive power of these bombs can only be roughly estimated, but there is no doubt that it would go far beyond all military conceptions. It appears likely that such bombs would be too heavy to be transported by airplane, but still they could be transported by boat and exploded in port with disastrous results.

Although at present it is uncertain whether a fast neutron reaction can be made to work, from now on this possibility will have to be constantly kept in mind in view of its far-reaching military consequences. Experiments have been devised for settling this important point, and it is solely a question of organization to ensure that such experiments shall be actually carried out.

Should the experiments show that a chain reaction will work with *fast* neutrons, it would then be highly advisable to arrange among scientists for withholding publications on this subject. An attempt to arrange for withholding publications on this subject has already been made early in March but was abandoned in spite of favourable response in this country and in England on account of the negative attitude of certain French laboratories. The experience gained in March would make it possible to revive this attempt whenever it should be necessary.

*Note* The Szilard letter and memorandum are reproduced from Fleming and Bailyn (1969), op cit, pp. 142–145. The Einstein letter is reproduced from Clark (1973), *Einstein*, Hodder.

# Appendix Five
# The Quebec Agreement: August 1943

**Articles of agreement governing collaboration between the authorities of the USA and UK in the matter of Tube Alloys**

Whereas it is vital to our common safety in the present War to bring the Tube Alloys project to fruition at the earliest moment; and whereas this may be more speedily achieved if all available British and American brains and resources are pooled; and whereas owing to war conditions it would be an improvident use of war resources to duplicate plants on a large scale on both sides of the Atlantic and therefore a far greater expense has fallen upon the United States;

It is agreed between us

First, that we will never use this agency against each other.

Secondly, that we will not use it against third parties without each other's consent.

Thirdly that we will not either of us communicate any information about Tube Alloys to third parties except by mutual consent.

Fourthly, that in view of the heavy burden of production falling upon the United States as the result of a wise division of war effort, the British Government recognise that any post-war advantages of an industrial or commercial character shall be dealt with as between the United States and Great Britain on terms specified by the President of the United States to the Prime Minister of Great Britain. The Prime Minister expressly disclaims any interest in these industrial and commercial aspects beyond what may be considered by the President of the United States to be fair and just and in harmony with the economic welfare of the world.

And Fifthly, that the following arrangements shall be made to ensure full and effective collaboration between the two countries in bringing the project to fruition:

(a) There shall be set up in Washington a Combined Policy Committee composed of:

| | |
|---|---|
| The Secretary of War | (United States) |
| Dr. Vannevar Bush | (United States) |
| Dr. James B. Conant | (United States) |

Field-Marshal Sir John Dill, GCB, CMG, DSO       (United Kingdom)
Colonel the Right Hon. J. J. Llewellin, CBE, MC, MP (United Kingdom)
The Honourable C. D. Howe                                      (Canada)

The functions of this Committee, subject to the control of the respective
Governments, will be:
  (1)  To agree from time to time upon the programme of work to be
       be carried out in the two countries.
  (2)  To keep all sections of the project under constant review.
  (3)  To allocate materials, apparatus and plant, in limited supply, in
       accordance with the requirements of the programme agreed by
       the Committee.
  (4)  To settle any questions which may arise on the interpretation or
       application of this Agreement.

(b) There shall be complete interchange of information and ideas on
all sections of the project between members of the Policy Committee
and their immediate technical advisers.

(c) In the field of scientific research and development there shall be
full and effective interchange of information and ideas between those
in the two countries engaged in the same sections of the field.

(d) In the field of design, construction and operation of large-scale
plants, interchange of information and ideas shall be regulated by such
ad hoc arrangements as may, in each section of the field, appear to be
necessary or desirable if the project is brought to fruition at the earliest
moment. Such ad hoc arrangements shall be subject to the approval of
the Policy Committee.

*Note* This text is reproduced from Gowing (1964), *Britain and Atomic Energy
1939–1945*, Macmillan, pp. 439–440.

# Appendix Six
# The Franck Report: June 11, 1945

## I. Preamble

The only reason to treat nuclear power differently from all the other developments in the field of physics is the possibility of its use as a means of political pressure in peace and sudden destruction in war. All present plans for the organization of research, scientific and industrial development, and publication in the field of nucleonics are conditioned by the political and military climate in which one expects those plans to be carried out. Therefore, in making suggestions for the postwar organization of nucleonics, a discussion of political problems cannot be avoided. The scientists on this Project do not presume to speak authoritatively on problems of national and international policy. However, we found ourselves, by the force of events during the last five years, in the position of a small group of citizens cognizant of a grave danger for the safety of this country as well as for the future of all other nations, of which the rest of mankind is unaware. We therefore feel it our duty to urge that the political problems, arising from the mastering of nuclear power, be recognized in all their gravity, and that appropriate steps be taken for their study and the preparation of necessary decisions. We hope that the creation of the Committee by the Secretary of War to deal with all aspects of nucleonics, indicates that these implications have been recognized by the government. We believe that our acquaintance with the scientific elements of the situation and prolonged preoccupation with its world-wide political implications, imposes on us the obligation to offer to the Committee some suggestions as to the possible solution of these grave problems.

Scientists have often before been accused of providing new weapons for the mutual destruction of nations, instead of improving their well-being. It is undoubtedly true that the discovery of flying, for example, has so far brought much more misery than enjoyment and profit to humanity  However, in the past, scientists could disclaim direct responsibility for the use to which mankind had put their disinterested discoveries. We feel compelled to take a more active stand now because the success which we have achieved in the development of nuclear power is fraught with infinitely greater dangers than were all the inventions of the past. All of us, familiar with the present state of nucleonics, live with the vision before our eyes of sudden destruction visited on our own country, of a Pearl Harbor disaster repeated in thousand-fold magnification in every one of our major cities.

In the past, science has often been able to provide also new methods of protection against new weapons of aggression it made possible, but it cannot promise such efficient protection against the destructive use of nuclear power. This protection can come only from the political organization of the world. Among all the arguments calling for an efficient international organization for peace, the existence of nuclear weapons is the most compelling one. *In the absence of an international authority which would make all resort to force in international conflicts impossible, nations could still be diverted from a path which must lead to total mutual destruction, by a specific international agreement barring a nuclear armaments race.*

## II. Prospects of Armaments Race

It could be suggested that the danger of destruction by nuclear weapons can be avoided — at least as far as this country is concerned — either by keeping our discoveries secret for an indefinite time, or else by developing our nucleonic armaments at such a pace that no other nations would think of attacking us from fear of overwhelming retaliation.

The answer to the first suggestion is that although we undoubtedly are at present ahead of the rest of the world in this field, the fundamental facts of nuclear power are a subject of common knowledge. British scientists know as much as we do about the basic wartime progress of nucleonics — if not of the specific processes used in our engineering developments — and the role which French nuclear physicists have played in the pre-war development of this field, plus their occasional contact with our Projects, will enable them to catch up rapidly, at least as far as basic scientific discoveries are concerned. German scientists, in whose discoveries the whole development of this field originated, apparently did not develop it during the war to the same extent to which this has been done in America; but to the last day of the European war, we were living in constant apprehension as to their possible achievements. The certainty that German scientists were working on this weapon and that their government would certainly have no scruples against using it when available, was the main motivation of the initiative which American scientists took in urging the development of nuclear power for military purposes on a large scale in this country. In Russia, too, the basic facts and implications of nuclear power were well understood in 1940, and the experience of Russian scientists in nuclear research is entirely sufficient to enable them to retrace our steps within a few years, even if we should make every attempt to conceal them. Furthermore, we should not expect too much success from attempts to keep basic information secret in peacetime, when scientists acquainted with the work on this and associated Projects will be scattered to many colleges and research institutions and many of them will continue to work on problems closely related to those on which our developments are based. In other words, even if we can retain our leadership in basic knowledge of nucleonics for a certain time by maintaining secrecy as to all results on this and associated Projects, it would be foolish to hope that this can protect us for more than a few years.

It may be asked whether we cannot prevent the development of military nucleonics in other countries by a monopoly on the raw materials of nuclear power. The answer is that even though the largest now known deposits of uranium ores are under the control of powers which belong to the "western" group (Canada, Belgium, and British India), the old deposits in Czechoslovakia are outside this sphere. Russia is known to be mining radium on its own territory; and even if we do not know the size of the deposits discovered so far in the USSR, the probability that no large reserves of uranium will be found in a country which covers $\frac{1}{5}$ of the land area of the earth (and whose sphere of influence takes in additional territory), is too small to serve as a basis for security. *Thus, we cannot hope to avoid a nuclear armament race either by keeping secret from the competing nations the basic scientific facts of nuclear power or by cornering the raw materials required for such a race.*

We now consider the second of the two suggestions made at the beginning of this section, and ask whether we could not feel ourselves safe in a race of nuclear armaments by virtue of our greater industrial potential, including greater diffusion of scientific and technical knowledge, greater volume and efficiency of our skilled labor corps, and greater experience of our management — all the factors whose importance has been so strikingly demonstrated in the conversion of this country into an arsenal of the Allied Nations in the present war. The answer is that all that these advantages can give us is the accumulation of a large number of bigger and better atomic bombs — and this only if we produce these bombs at the maximum of our capacity in peace time, and do not rely on conversion of a peace-time nucleonics industry to military production after the beginning of hostilities.

However, such a quantitative advantage in reserves of bottled destructive power will not make us safe from sudden attack. Just because a potential enemy will be afraid of being "outnumbered and outgunned," the temptation for him may be overwhelming to attempt a sudden unprovoked blow — particularly if he should suspect us of harboring aggressive intentions against his security or his sphere of influence. In no other type of warfare does the advantage lie so heavily with the aggressor. He can place his "infernal machines" in advance in all our major cities and explode them simultaneously, thus destroying a major part of our industry and a large part of our population, aggregated in densely populated metropolitan districts. Our possibilities of retaliation — even if retaliation should be considered adequate compensation for the loss of millions of lives and destruction of our largest cities — will be greatly handicapped because we must rely on aerial transportation of the bombs, and also because we may have to deal

with an enemy whose industry and population are dispersed over a
large territory.

In fact, if the race for nuclear armaments is allowed to develop, the
only apparent way in which our country can be protected from the
paralyzing effects of a sudden attack is by dispersal of those industries
which are essential for our war effort and dispersal of the populations
of our major metropolitan cities. As long as nuclear bombs remain
scarce (i.e., as long as uranium and thorium remain the only basic
materials for their fabrication), efficient dispersal of our industry and
the scattering of our metropolitan population will considerably
decrease the temptation to attack us by nuclear weapons.

Ten years hence, it may be that atomic bombs containing perhaps
20 kg of active material can be detonated at 6% efficiency, and thus
each have an effect equal to that of 20,000 tons of TNT. One of these
bombs could then destroy something like 3 square miles of an urban
area. Atomic bombs containing a larger quantity of active material but
still weighing less than one ton may be expected to be available within
ten years which could destroy over ten square miles of a city. A nation
able to assign 10 tons of atomic explosives for the preparation of a
sneak attack on this country, can then hope to achieve the destruction
of all industry and most of the population in an area from 500 square
miles upwards. If no choice of targets, with a total area of five hundred
square miles of American territory, contains a large enough fraction of
the nation's industry and population to make their destruction a
crippling blow to the nation's war potential and its ability to defend
itself, then the attack will not pay, and may not be undertaken. At
present, one could easily select in this country a hundred areas of five
square miles each whose simultaneous destruction would be a staggering
blow to the nation. Since the area of the United States is about three
million square miles, it should be possible to scatter its industrial and
human resources in such a way as to leave no 500 square miles important
enough to serve as a target for nuclear attack.

We are fully aware of the staggering difficulties involved in such a
radical change in the social and economic structure of our nation. We
felt, however, that the dilemma had to be stated, to show what kind of
alternative methods of protection will have to be considered if no
successful international agreement is reached. It must be pointed out
that in this field we are in a less favorable position than nations which
are either now more diffusely populated and whose industries are more
scattered, or whose governments have unlimited power over the movement of population and the location of industrial plants.

If no efficient international agreement is achieved, the race for
nuclear armaments will be on in earnest not later than the morning
after our first demonstration of the existence of nuclear weapons.
After this, it might take other nations three or four years to overcome
our present head start, and eight or ten years to draw even with us if

we continue to do intensive work in this field. This might be all the time we would have to bring about the regroupment of our population and industry. Obviously, no time should be lost in inaugurating a study of this problem by experts.

## III. Prospects of Agreement

The consequences of nuclear warfare, and the type of measures which would have to be taken to protect a country from total destruction by nuclear bombing, must be as abhorrent to other nations as to the United States. England, France, and the smaller nations of the European continent, with their congeries of people and industries, would be in a particularly desperate situation in the face of such a threat. Russia and China are the only great nations at present which could survive a nuclear attack. However, even though these countries may value human life less than the peoples of Western Europe and America, and even though Russia, in particular, has an immense space over which its vital industries could be dispersed and a government which can order this dispersion the day it is convinced that such a measure is necessary — there is no doubt that Russia will shudder at the possibility of a sudden disintegration of Moscow and Leningrad and of its new industrial cities in the Urals and Siberia. Therefore, only lack of mutual *trust*, and not lack of *desire* for agreement, can stand in the path of an efficient agreement for the prevention of nuclear warfare. The achievement of such an agreement will thus essentially depend on the integrity of intentions and readiness to sacrifice the necessary fraction of one's own sovereignty, by all the parties to the agreement.

From this point of view, the way in which the nuclear weapons now being secretly developed in this country are first revealed to the world appears to be of great, perhaps fateful importance.

One possible way — which may particularly appeal to those who consider nuclear bombs primarily as a secret weapon developed to help win the present war — is to use them without warning on an appropriately selected object in Japan. It is doubtful whether the first available bombs, of comparatively low efficiency and small size, will be sufficient to break the will or ability of Japan to resist, especially given the fact that the major cities like Tokyo, Nagoya, Osaka and Kobe already will largely have been reduced to ashes by the slower processes of ordinary aerial bombing. Although important tactical results undoubtedly can be achieved by a sudden introduction of nuclear weapons, we nevertheless think that the question of the use of the very first available atomic bombs in the Japanese war should be weighed very carefully, not only by military authorities, but by the highest political leadership of this country. If we consider international agreement on total prevention of nuclear warfare as the paramount objective, and believe that it can be achieved, this kind of introduction of atomic weapons to the world may easily destroy all our chances of success. Russia, and even allied countries which bear less mistrust of our ways and intentions, as well as neutral countries may be deeply shocked. It may be very difficult to persuade the world that a nation which was capable of secretly preparing and suddenly releasing a weapon as indiscriminate as the rocket bomb and a million times more destructive, is to be trusted in its proclaimed desire of having such weapons abolished by international agreement. We have large accumulations of poison gas, but do not use them, and recent polls have shown that public opinion in this country would disapprove of such a use even if it would accelerate the winning of the Far Eastern war. It is true that some irrational element in mass psychology makes gas poisoning more revolting than blasting by explosives, even though gas warfare is in no way more "inhuman" than the war of bombs and bullets. Nevertheless, it is not at all certain that American public opinion, if it could be enlightened as to the effect of atomic explosives, would approve of our own country being the first to introduce such an indiscriminate method of wholesale destruction of civilian life.

Thus, from the "optimistic" point of view — looking forward to an international agreement on the prevention of nuclear warfare — the military advantages and the saving of American lives achieved by the sudden use of atomic bombs against Japan may be outweighed by the ensuing loss of confidence and by a wave of horror and repulsion sweeping over the rest of the world and perhaps even dividing public opinion at home.

*From this point of view, a demonstration of the new weapon might best be made, before the eyes of representatives of all the United Nations, on the desert or a barren island.* The best possible atmosphere for the achievement of an international agreement could be achieved if America could say to the world, "You see what sort of a weapon we had but did not use. We are ready to renounce its use in the future if other nations join us in this renunciation and agree to the establishment of an efficient international control."

After such demonstration the weapon might perhaps be used against Japan if the sanction of the United Nations (and of public opinion at home) were obtained, perhaps after a preliminary ultimatum to Japan to surrender or at least to evacuate certain regions as an alternative to their total destruction. This may sound fantastic, but in nuclear weapons we have something entirely new in order of magnitude of destructive power, and if we want to capitalize fully on the advantage their possession gives us, we must use new and imaginative methods.

It must be stressed that if one takes the pessimistic point of view and discounts the possibility of an effective international control over nuclear weapons at the present time, then the advisability of an early use of nuclear bombs against Japan becomes even more doubtful —

quite independently of any humanitarian considerations. If an international agreement is not concluded immediately after the first demonstration, this will mean a flying start toward an unlimited armaments race. If this race is inevitable, we have every reason to delay its beginning as long as possible in order to increase our head start still further. It took us three years, roughly, under forced draft of wartime urgency, to complete the first stage of production of nuclear explosives — that based on the separation of the rare fissionable isotope $U^{235}$, or its utilization for the production of an equivalent quantity of another fissionable element. This stage required large-scale, expensive constructions and laborious procedures. We are now on the threshold of the second stage — that of converting into fissionable material the comparatively abundant common isotopes of thorium and uranium. This stage probably requires no elaborate plans and may provide us in about five or six years with a really substantial stockpile of atomic bombs. Thus it is to our interest to delay the beginning of the armaments race at least until the successful termination of this second stage. The benefit to the nation, and the saving of American lives in the future, achieved by renouncing an early demonstration of nuclear bombs and letting the other nations come into the race only reluctantly, on the basis of guesswork and without definite knowledge that the "thing does work," may far outweigh the advantages to be gained by the immediate use of the first and comparatively inefficient bombs in the war against Japan. On the other hand, it may be argued that without an early demonstration it may prove difficult to obtain adequate support for further intensive development of nucleonics in this country and that thus the time gained for the postponement of an open armaments race will not be properly used. Furthermore one may suggest that other nations are now, or will soon be, not entirely unaware of our present achievements, and that consequently the postponement of a demonstration may serve no useful purpose as far as the avoidance of an armaments race is concerned, and may only create additional mistrust, thus worsening rather than improving the chances of an ultimate accord on the international control of nuclear explosives.

Thus, if the prospects of an agreement will be considered poor in the immediate future, the pros and cons of an early revelation of our possession of nuclear weapons to the world — not only by their actual use against Japan, but also by a prearranged demonstration — must be carefully weighed by the supreme political and military leadership of the country, and the decision should not be left to military tacticians alone.

One may point out that scientists themselves have initiated the development of this "secret weapon" and it is therefore strange that they should be reluctant to try it out on the enemy as soon as it is available. The answer to this question was given before — the compelling reason for creating this weapon with such speed was our fear that Germany had the technical skill necessary to develop such a weapon, and that the German government had no moral restraints regarding its use.

Another argument which could be quoted in favor of using atomic bombs as soon as they are available is that so much taxpayers' money has been invested in these Projects that the Congress and the American public will demand a return for their money. The attitude of American public opinion, mentioned earlier, in the matter of the use of poison gas against Japan, shows that one can expect the American public to understand that it is sometimes desirable to keep a weapon in readiness for use only in extreme urgency; and as soon as the potentialities of nuclear weapons are revealed to the American people, one can be sure that they will support all attempts to make the use of such weapons impossible.

Once this is achieved, the large installations and the accumulation of explosive material at present earmarked for potential military use will become available for important peace-time developments, including power production, large engineering undertakings, and mass production of radioactive materials. In this way, the money spent on wartime development of nucleonics may become a boon for the peacetime development of national economy.

## IV. Methods of International Control

We now consider the question of how an effective international control of nuclear armaments can be achieved. This is a difficult problem, but we think it soluble. It requires study by statesmen and international lawyers, and we can offer only some preliminary suggestions for such a study.

Given mutual trust and willingness on all sides to give up a certain part of their sovereign rights, by admitting international control of certain phases of national economy, the control could be exercised (alternatively or simultaneously) on two different levels.

The first and perhaps simplest way is to ration the raw materials — primarily the uranium ores. Production of nuclear explosives begins with the processing of large quantities of uranium in large isotope separation plants or huge production piles. The amounts of ore taken out of the ground at different locations could be controlled by resident agents of the international Control Board, and each nation could be allotted only an amount which would make large scale separation of fissionable isotopes impossible.

Such a limitation would have the drawback of making impossible also the development of nuclear power for peace-time purposes. However, it need not prevent the production of radioactive elements on a scale sufficient to revolutionalize the industrial, scientific and technical use of these materials, and would thus not eliminate the main benefits which nucleonics promises to bring to mankind.

An agreement on a higher level, involving more mutual trust and understanding, would be to allow unlimited production, but keep exact bookkeeping on the fate of each pound of uranium mined. Some difficulty with this method of control will arise in the second stage of production, when one pound of pure fissionable isotope will be used again and again to produce additional fissionable material from thorium. These could be overcome by extending control to the mining and use of thorium, even though the commercial use of this metal may cause complications.

If check is kept on the conversion of uranium and thorium ore into pure fissionable materials, the question arises as to how to prevent accumulation of large quantities of such materials in the hands of one or several nations. Accumulations of this kind could be rapidly converted into atomic bombs if a nation should break away from international control. It has been suggested that a compulsory denaturation of pure fissionable isotopes may be agreed upon by diluting them, after production, with suitable isotopes to make them useless for military purposes, while retaining their usefulness for power engines.

One thing is clear: any international agreement on prevention of nuclear armaments much be backed by actual and efficient controls. No paper agreement can be sufficient since neither this nor any other nation can stake its whole existence on trust in other nations' signatures. Every attempt to impede the international control agencies would have to be considered equivalent to denunciation of the agreement.

It hardly needs stressing that we as scientists believe that any systems of control envisaged should leave as much freedom for the peacetime development of nucleonics as is consistent with the safety of the world.


## Summary

The development of nuclear power not only constitutes an important addition to the technological and military power of the United States, but also creates grave political and economic problems for the future of this country.

Nuclear bombs cannot possibly remain a "secret weapon" at the exclusive disposal of this country for more than a few years. The scientific facts on which their construction is based are well known to scientists of other countries. Unless an effective international control of nuclear explosives is instituted, a race for nuclear armaments is certain to ensue following the first revelation of our possession of nuclear weapons to the world. Within ten years other countries may have nuclear bombs, each of which, weighing less than a ton, could destroy

an urban area of more than ten square miles. In the war to which such
an armaments race is likely to lead, the United States, with its agglo-
meration of population and industry in comparatively few metropolitan
districts, will be at a disadvantage compared to nations whose population
and industry are scattered over large areas.

We believe that these considerations make the use of nuclear bombs
for an early unannounced attack against Japan inadvisable. If the
United States were to be the first to release this new means of indiscriminate destruction upon mankind, she would sacrifice public support
throughout the world, precipitate the race for armaments, and prejudice
the possibility of reaching an international agreement on the future
control of such weapons.

Much more favorable conditions for the eventual achievement of
such an agreement could be created if nuclear bombs were first revealed
to the world by a demonstration in an appropriately selected uninhabited
area.

In case chances for the establishment of an effective international
control of nuclear weapons should have to be considered slight at the
present time, then not only the use of these weapons against Japan, but
even their early demonstration, may be contrary to the interests of this
country. A postponement of such a demonstration will have in this case
the advantage of delaying the beginning of the nuclear armaments race
as long as possible. If, during the time gained, ample support can be
made available for further development of the field in this country, the
postponement will substantially increase the lead which we have established during the present war, and our position in an armament race or
in any later attempt at international agreement would thus be
strengthened.

On the other hand, if no adequate public support for the development of nucleonics will be available without a demonstration, the
postponement of the latter may be deemed inadvisable, because enough
information might leak out to cause other nations to start the armament race, in which we would then be at a disadvantage. There is also
the possibility that the distrust of other nations may be aroused if they
know that we are conducting a development under cover of secrecy,
and that this will make it more difficult eventually to reach an agreement with them.

If the government should decide in favor of an early demonstration
of nuclear weapons, it will then have the possibility of taking into
account the public opinion of this country and of the other nations
before deciding whether these weapons should be used in the war
against Japan. In this way, other nations may assume a share of
responsibility for such a fateful decision.

To sum up, we urge that the use of nuclear bombs in this war be
considered as a problem of long-range national policy rather than of
military expediency, and that this policy be directed primarily to the

achievement of an agreement permitting an effective international control of the means of nuclear warfare.

The vital importance of such a control for our country is obvious from the fact that the only effective alternative method of protecting this country appears to be a dispersal of our major cities and essential industries.

J. Franck, *Chairman*
D. J. Hughes
J. J. Nickson
E. Rabinowitch
G. T. Seaborg
J. C. Stearns
L. Szilard

*Note* This text is reproduced from Smith (1965), *A Peril and a Hope*, University of Chicago Press, pp. 560–572.